Endpapers: Left hand page: Part of the unique sheet of Penny Black stamps held at the National Postal Museum. (See page 96) Right hand page: A montage of penny stamps featuring each of the six monarchs since 1840.

Opposite: The original Fleet Street presses of Perkins, Bacon and Co, used to print the Penny Black stamps. Five presses, each able to print 800 sheets of 240 stamps in 24 hours, operated night and day in 1840 to meet the demand.

FIRST POST

A postbus calls at a rural sub-office in Cornwall. By Ben Maile.

First Post

FROM PENNY BLACK
TO THE PRESENT DAY

PETER DAVIES and **BEN MAILE**

The Post Office
Quiller Press

First published 1990
by Quiller Press Ltd.,
46 Lillie Road,
London SW6 1TN

Copyright © 1990 The Post Office
New drawings and paintings: Ben Maile

Designed by Linda Wade

Typeset by Bookworm Typesetting,
Manchester
Printed in Great Britain by
Butler & Tanner Ltd,
Frome and London

ISBN 1 870948 43 2

Acknowledgements

The authors wish to acknowledge the
invaluable and unstinting help of Jean
Farrugia, the Post Office Archivist,
and Peter Howe, the Photographic
Manager, whose influence covers most
of the book, and the many Post Office
people who have helped with specific
chapters, particularly: Ron Clatworthy, Tony Gammons, Mike Goss, Mike
Hall, Mike Holmes, Mike Jenkins,
Douglas Muir, Alex Obradovic, Stuart
Pretty, Ian Randle, Mavis Riley, Barry
Robinson, Phil Rogers, Andrew Scarborough and Martin Stephenson.

Contents

Herbert Evans, the last of London's river postmen, delivered to ships moored in the Pool of London from 1914 until the service ended with his retirement in 1952. This was also the end of 142 years of unbroken service in the same post by five generations of the Evans family. Herbert Evans's day began at the Eastern district sorting office where he had to check the registered position of the ships before starting his waterborne deliveries.

Introduction

With the introduction in 1840 of uniform penny postage – and the world's first postage stamp – the Royal Mail became a central part of British life. Literacy flourished as never before, and a more literate workforce helped industry – and life generally – to flourish with it.

The Post Office flourished too, its letter delivery role expanding to encompass money orders, savings, a parcels post, telegraphs, telephones, banking ... The local post office became the hub of its community.

Transport progressed from horses and sailing ships to jet planes and hovercraft – and the Royal Mail has been closely involved with them all. As the railways spread their net across the country, the Post Office was an early and influential customer.

Through the dramas of war the Post Office was always at the centre, keeping communication lifelines – operational and personal – open, often with temporary staff as its young men joined active units.

Britain's Post Office in the 1990s is very much larger and vastly more diverse than the one Rowland Hill tackled in 1840.

Overall the Post Office Corporation continues to set standards and policies for its three postal businesses, and service to the customer remains the key.

The Royal Mail's priority is to continue to improve its collection and delivery services. Already, the start of the 1990s has seen the reintroduction of Sunday collections and more detailed information to customers on the latest posting times for next-day delivery in different parts of the

London's Lombard Street, hub of the mail coach network until the 1830s when St Martin's-le-Grand became the starting point of the spectacular nightly exodus. By Ben Maile.

country.

Parcelforce is a more autonomous business in the 1990s than it has ever been, with special sorting offices and distribution networks operating services that include guaranteed 24-hour and 48-hour business deliveries as well as Datapost.

Post Office Counters is also entering the 1990s with confidence, attracting customers to its counters by speeding service, improving choice and developing its role as a High Street shop.

This is the story of the British Post Office across 150 years, from that day in 1840 when it led the world by making its service accessible and affordable to the public at large, to the present day, much more commercial organisation determined to maintain its world lead into the next century.

It is a dramatic, almost larger-than-life story of an organisation that touches everyone's life, covering a period of progress unprecedented in world history.

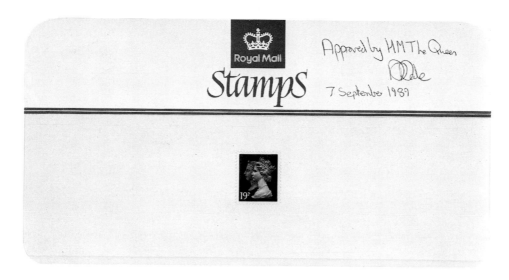

The sample or "essay" of the 150th Anniversary stamp approved by the Queen in September 1989 (before the price increase of 2 October). Five values – 15p (blue), 20p (black), 29p, 34p and 37p – went on sale in January 1990.

Sir Rowland Hill

Chapter 1
The Penny Black Era

Wednesday 6 May 1840 is the most significant date in the history of the world's postal services. It is the date the Penny Black, the world's first adhesive postage stamp, was first accepted as payment for carrying a letter. It heralded a postal revolution.

That year, for the first time, there was a standard price for posting a letter from and to anywhere in the kingdom. Also for the first time, payment in advance for letter delivery would be the norm rather than the exception and, most significant of all, the price was brought within the means of the public as a whole.

This transformation was down to one man, Rowland Hill.

In 1837 this Kidderminster-born former school teacher was 41 and he had already made his mark as a successful innovator in fields as diverse as printing and road making. But in January that year he set about changing the world. He produced and published a paper which spelled out in detail what he thought was wrong with the postal services of the day and how they should be put right.

He was not alone in criticising the existing set-up. For the best part of 200 years the Post Office had been in business to gather in the largest possible revenue. Charges were based not on costs but on the requirements of the Treasury. But even so, most of the high and sometimes illogical costs were eaten up by the cumbersome bureaucracy involved in collecting the revenue. These included:

Right: Ben Maile's impression of an early letter carrier.

1 charges based on one sheet of paper, folded and sealed with wax; two sheets doubled the price;

2 a price dependant on distance: up to 15 miles; 15 to 20; 20 to 30; 30 to 50 and so on;

3 the recording of every letter handed in;

4 a myriad of exceptions – an extra penny if the route was over the Menai Bridge, a ha'penny more for any letter carried in Scotland by a carriage with more than two wheels...

UNIFORM
Penny Postage

" It is not the cause of faction, or of party, or of an individual, but the common interest of every man in Britain." *— Junius.*

A PETITION
Lies here for Signatures
ONLY ONE DAY

For signing the PETITION, which must be

PRESENTED ON FRIDAY

Ma   n without a moment's delay!

Above: The pressure for postal reform grew throughout the 1830s. The petition this poster advertised in 1839 was organised by the Mercantile Committee, a powerful group of merchants set up to campaign for postal reform. Within a year Rowland Hill's reforms were introduced and with them (right) the world's first adhesive postage stamp, the Penny Black.

Left: How to get postal value in the days when sending two sheets doubled the price.

The complications combined with the cost led to people using all kinds of enterprising dodges to get the better of the system.

People would write their letter in the normal way then turn the page on its side and write vertically across their earlier lines. A group of businessmen even arranged to send letters to people in the same district by writing them all on one large sheet of paper, charged as a single letter. At the far end the letter was divided into its separate parts and delivered by hand.

Often a letter to, say, Scotland would be carried all the way for 13½ pence, payable on delivery, only for the addressee, having spotted the handwriting and so knowing that the writer was alive and well, to decline to accept the letter.

Another problem was that the poorly paid letter carrier would often be returning with a fair amount of cash in payment for postage and could either be tempted to spend some of the money and get into debt or he might be attacked and robbed.

So it was costly, it was inefficient and as a result it was hampering communications and slowing the spread of literacy and the expansion of trade. As people moved from their home villages to the new industrial centres they soon lost touch with relatives and friends. Industry, particularly, needed a literate labour force and a less costly medium for sending out price lists, bills, receipts.

As Rowland Hill eloquently pointed out, the system was riddled with problems and ripe for reform.

In his pioneering 1837 paper 'Post Office Reform – its Importance and Practicability' Rowland Hill was able to show that a day's batch of mail from London to Edinburgh cost the Post Office less than a ha'penny a letter to deliver, yet the postage charged was 27 times that.

The service could be run more efficiently and economically, he said, if the postage was charged in advance at a uniform rate based on weight. Postage could be a penny for each letter or packet weighing up to half an ounce and a further penny for each additional half-ounce. Forget all this nonsense about numbers of sheets of paper and distances involved.

His main proposals for the prepayment of the postage were by cash at letter receiving offices or by the sale of official prepaid stamped stationery –

A typical, perhaps smarter than average, letter carrier of the early 1800s.

TO ALL POSTMASTERS
AND
SUB-POSTMASTERS.

GENERAL POST OFFICE,
25th April, 1840.

IT has been decided that Postage Stamps are to be brought into use forthwith, and as it will be necessary that every such Stamp should be cancelled at the Post Office or Sub-Post Office where the Letter bearing the same may be posted, I herewith forward, for your use, an *Obliterating Stamp*, with which you will efface the Postage Stamp upon every Letter despatched from your Office. *Red Composition* must be used for this purpose, and I annex directions for making it, with an Impression of the Stamp.

As the Stamps will come into operation by the *6th of May*, I must desire you will not fail to provide yourself with the necessary supply of Red Composition by that time.

Directions for Preparing the Red Stamping Composition.

1 lb. Printer's Red Ink.
1 Pint Linseed Oil.
Half-pint of the Droppings of Sweet Oil.
To be well mixed.

By Command,

W. L. MABERLY,
SECRETARY.

Above: The notice to postmasters, enclosed with an "obliterating stamp", explaining how to cancel the Penny Black. It did not work well, hence the switch to the Penny Red with black cancellation.

William Mulready intended his design of prepaid stationery – envelope and letter sheet – to convey the widespread benefits of cheaper postage emanating from Great Britain. The design was "much approved" by the Royal Academy.

Below: One of a number of lampoons of the Mulready design.

envelopes or foldable sheets. No thought, at this stage, of separate stamps to stick on private stationery.

A little later that year, responding to an enquiry into his proposals, he suggested the possibility of using a bit of paper just large enough to bear the stamped impression, and covered at the back with a 'glutinous wash' which might, with the application of a little moisture . . .

The world's first postage stamp was on its way.

The penny post itself was not new. Many British cities had their own penny post but only for mail posted and delivered locally. Each letter was franked at the office of posting, with black ink used when payment was due on receipt and red ink to show the letter had been prepaid.

The uniform prepaid penny post actually began on 10 January 1840, but it was not until Friday, 1 May, that the stamps and prepaid stationery went on sale, ready for their official use in the post the following Wednesday.

Some one-and-a-half million were printed and distributed in time for the launch along with a similar vast quantity of the prepaid envelopes or Mulreadys as they were called after

their designer, Sir William Mulready RA. They went to post offices (the central points where mail bags were received), to local letter receiving houses and to reputable shops that were licensed to sell them.

Rowland Hill was not alone in expecting the official prepaid stationery – the Mulreadys – to be the main method of prepayment. But the public hated them, they were ridiculed in the press and people simply bought their own envelopes and used the new penny stamps.

While the Penny Black was well received compared with the lampooning of the Mulreadys, it did not escape completely. A letter to *The Times* described it as 'a libel upon the fair countenance of our Queen', and at the other end of the newspaper scale a weekly scandal sheet called 'The Town' offered this:

> You must kiss our fair Queen,
>   or her pictures, that's clear
> Or the gummy medallion will
>   never adhere;
> You will not kiss her hand, you
>   will readily find
> But actually kiss little Vickey's
>   behind.

In fact the Penny Black has stood the test of time as an exceptional

A Penny Black with the red cancellation and (below) the Penny Red cancelled with black ink.

By Command of the Postmaster General.

NOTICE to the PUBLIC.

Rapid Delivery of Letters.

GENERAL POST OFFICE,
May, 1849.

The Postmaster General is desirous of calling attention to the greater rapidity of delivery which would obviously be consequent on the general adoption of *Street-door Letter Boxes, or Slits,* in private dwelling houses, and indeed wherever the Postman is at present kept waiting.

He hopes that householders will not object to the means by which, at a very moderate expense, they may secure so desirable an advantage to themselves, to their neighbours, and to the Public Service.

Above: The 1849 poster appealing to the public to put letter slits in their doors to speed delivery. The widespread lack of numbering on houses was another problem for the Post Office and many street names were duplicated.

example of miniature design, engraving and printing, setting a British tradition of sustained excellence in this art.

The Penny Black lasted just ten months. In that time some 68 million stamps were printed – and large stockpiles of prepaid stationery withdrawn and destroyed!

On 10 February 1841 Penny Red stamps went on sale, replacing the Penny Black. The switch came because the Post Office was getting worried that its stamp cancellations (in red) were not showing up on the black stamps and people could use them over again. So after much experiment they reversed the position – red stamps and black cancellation.

The switch cost very little: with no change in design they were able to use the same printing plates. The design lasted with only minor variations for 40 years, when the original printers, Perkins Bacon, finally lost the contract. De La Rue took over from 1 January 1880.

The 68 million Penny Blacks sold in the ten months from May 1840 represented a spectacular growth in postal activity compared with previous years, but it was just the start. Not even the visionary Rowland Hill could have imagined today's daily postings of 54 million letters.

He still had the problem of getting local authorities to number the houses and of distinguishing between streets with the same name, not to mention persuading householders to put slits in their front doors so letters could be delivered without the letter carrier having to knock and wait.

Hill's reforms were transforming British life. Literacy, and with it education generally, improved. Business and commerce flourished, and families divided by distance were kept in touch.

The world followed. Brazil was the quickest, introducing postage stamps nationally in 1843, and the United States, Russia, France, Spain and Portugal were among the many countries to follow suit in the next decade.

In the words of Mr Gladstone, Rowland Hill's reforms had 'run like wildfire through the civilised world: never perhaps was a local invention and improvement applied in the lifetime of its author to the advantages of such vast multitudes of his fellow creatures.'

Chapter 2
Before the Penny Black

In 1985 the Post Office celebrated the 350th anniversary of the Royal Mail as a public service. The festivities centred on Bagshot where Prince Charles travelled with commemorative mail on a horse-drawn mail coach.

It was in Bagshot on 31 July 1635 that King Charles I issued a proclamation allowing his subjects to use his Royal Mail.

What exactly did Charles I hand over to his people? Not a great deal. There were just a few permanent postal routes radiating from London each with a series of staging 'posts'. These were inns where the innkeeper also maintained stables. He was the

Right: A wave from Prince Charles as he arrives at Bagshot for the Royal Mail's 350th anniversary celebrations in 1985.

By the King.

A Proclamation for the ſetling of the Letter
Office of England and Scotland.

 Hereas to this time there hath beene no certaine or conſtant enter-courſe betweene the Kingdomes of England and Scotland, His Maiesty hath beene graciouſly pleaſed, to command His ſeruant Thomas Witherings Eſquire, His Maiesties Post-maſter of England for forraigne parts, to ſetle a running Post, or two, to run night and day betweene Edenburgh in Scotland, and the City of London, to goe thither, and come backe againe in ſixe dayes, and to take with them all ſuch Letters as ſhall be directed to any Post-towne, or any place neere any Post-towne in the ſaid Roade, which Letters to be left at the Post-houſe, or ſome other houſe, as the ſaid Thomas Witherings ſhall thinke conuenient: And By Posts to be placed at ſeuerall places out of the ſaid Roade, to run and bring in, and carry out of the ſaid Roades the Letters from Lincolne, Hull, and other places, as there ſhall be occaſion, and anſweres to be brought againe accordingly; And to pay Post for the carrying and recarrying of the ſaid Letters, Two pence the ſingle Letter, if vnder foureſcore Miles; And betweene foureſcore, and one hundred and fourty Miles, Foure pence; If aboue a hundred and fourty Miles, then ſixe pence; and vpon the borders of Scotland, and in Scotland, Eight pence: If there be two, three, foure, or fiue Letters in one Packet, or more, Then to pay according to the bigneſſe of the ſaid Packet, after the rate as before; which money for Post as before, is to be paid vpon the receiuing and deliuery of the ſaid Letters here in London.

The opening section of Charles I proclamation making his Royal Mail available to his subjects.

postmaster, commissioned to provide the King's messenger with a fresh horse for the next stage of his journey.

Any other routes the king might need were set up as required, often as the court moved about the country. Selected innkeepers along the routes became postmasters for as long as the king needed them.

As for the rest of the population, it was a more parochial world in those days so there was not a great deal of demand. Merchants either made their own private arrangements or used commercial carriers.

After the Royal Proclamation – aimed at creating revenue – permanent routes from London were quickly established to Dover, Edinburgh, Holyhead, Plymouth, Bristol and, a little later, Harwich and Great Yarmouth.

The King's messengers were replaced by post-boys: the same job but not quite so smart. They had no official uniform but could be recognised by their tin hats and big boots stuffed with hay to keep their feet warm.

Also unlike the King's messenger, each had his own patch, riding between 'posts' and delivering the mail to the postmaster who would hand it on to the next mounted post-boy, like a relay race. But the race was a slow one over poor roads, and six miles an hour was good going.

As well as speeding the mail, the postmaster accepted letters brought in for posting by people from the

A 17th century mounted post-boy arriving at Dover. (A 1955 drawing for the Post Office Magazine by E A Oldman.)

many communities off the beaten track. In those days many people had quite a journey to post a letter.

It was not until 1720 that these main postal arteries centred on London began to be augmented nation-wide by routes which formed links between them. The expansion of these routes, called cross-posts, was the brainchild of Ralph Allen, postmaster of Bath and already manager of a cross-post between Exeter and Chester. By the time of his death in 1764 Allen's elaborate network of cross-posts had transformed the postal service.

So the links between the towns and cities were developing well. But what about the local deliveries within these centres? Back in the early 1680s the Post Office, still concentrating on maintaining and extending its trunk links, had made no attempt to provide a mail service for Londoners. It was as easy to send a letter to Dover as it was to get one across London. It was a crying need and an enterprising London merchant called William Dockwra decided to do something about it.

He it was who in 1680 created the very first prepaid penny post. That was his charge for the collection and delivery of local letters and parcels

9

(weighing up to 1lb). He divided London into districts, each with its own sorting office, and set up hundreds of letter receiving offices. It was a soar-away success – but, for Dockwra at least, it was short-lived.

Within two years his service was closed down as an infringement of the Royal post monopoly, the profits of which went to James, Duke of York,

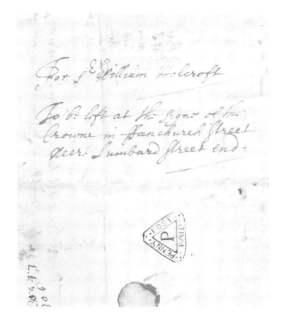

A letter delivered by William Dockwra's London Penny Post. The "P" of the postmark indicates that it went through the St Paul's office. The Post Office used similar postmarks when it took over Dockwra's service. The complicated address is an indication of the problems in the days before house numbering.

later King James II. However, it soon reopened, this time as part of the Post Office.

More than 80 years later – in 1765 – an Act was passed allowing local penny post networks in key towns outside London, but nothing happened very quickly. After about eight years one started in Dublin, then a private service was launched in Edinburgh. But it was not for another 20 years that the big centres in England got their own local penny post systems. Manchester took the lead in 1793 and in that same year Edinburgh's became an official service.

Letter receiving houses sprang up locally. The tendency was to move away from inns, which women, particularly, did not like, and there was less need to be associated with stables. They began to be established instead in reputable local shops, or perhaps the local schoolmaster would take on the task. The letter carriers – on foot or horse, or even with a cart – had regular routes for collection and delivery to the receiving houses, where the local people could post or collect their mail. These walks could be as long as 16 miles.

The postal network that was to handle Rowland Hill's uniform penny post was taking shape. But to date it was not getting much faster. The relays of horse-backed post boys had changed little over the 150 years since the days of Charles I.

There was one significant development, but it was not for the better. The post-boys were becoming frequent targets for highway robbers. Around 1770 not a day went by without at least one mail robbery. People sending money through the post were even advised to cut bank notes in half and send each half separately.

The Post Office tried all sorts of things: a wooden carriage carrying an iron chest; an iron coach that took two horses to pull it – even military escorts. Finally they found the answer: the mail coach.

Here's a good quiz question: What do the postal network of the late 18th century and the mail coaches that were to use that network have in common? The answer: Bath.

The city where Ralph Allen, creator of the cross-posts network, had been postmaster was also the home of a young theatre proprietor called John Palmer.

Mail coaches were Palmer's idea. He had acquired a second theatre in

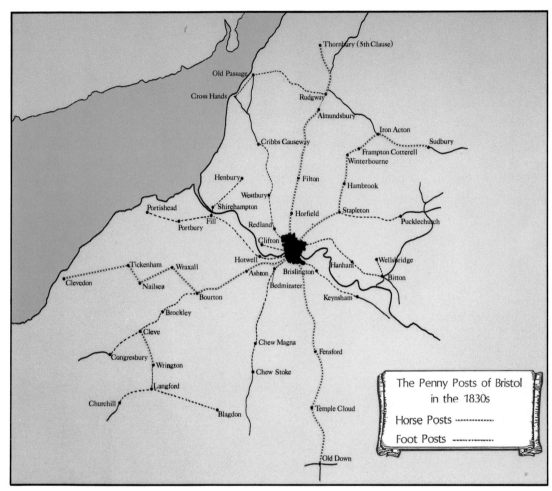

Map of Bristol's local penny post area around 1830 showing the considerable distances involved.

Letter carriers, many in their early teens, would often have regular walks of up to 16 miles a day.

Bristol and had introduced a regular service of post-chaises to carry actors and props between the two cities. Convinced that what had worked for the theatre would also work for the mail, Palmer sold his theatre interests and headed for London to put his ideas to the Post Office.

He pointed out that while a modern stage could travel from Bristol to London in 17 hours, the mail took two days. Properly organised he said, the mail could be carried by coach in 16 hours.

The Post Office was sceptical, but none other than William Pitt, then Chancellor of the Exchequer, gave Palmer the chance to put his ideas to the test. The coach left the Swan Tavern in Bristol at 4pm on 2 August 1784, called at the Three Tuns in Bath and arrived at the Swan with Two Necks in London 16 hours later – exactly on time.

Within a year mail coaches were speeding the Royal Mail to Norwich, Liverpool and Leeds, quickly followed by services to Dover, Portsmouth, Poole, Exeter, Gloucester, Worcester, Holyhead and Carlisle. By 1786 the 400 miles from London to Edinburgh were being covered in 60 hours, 25 hours less than the relay of mounted post-boys.

And it was a great deal safer. As recommended by Palmer, every mail coach carried a Post Office guard armed with a cutlass, a brace of pistols and a blunderbuss. He also had a military-style uniform: scarlet coat with blue lapels and gold braid, and a black hat with a gold band. A time-piece, locked and regulated in London, kept a check on the strict Post

John Palmer the theatrical impressario turned mail-coach pioneer, who was later put in charge of mail operations.

Office timetable, and he had a post horn to warn travellers and tollgate keepers to make way for the Royal Mail which had priority over other traffic.

In the 60 years of the mail coach era there is only one recorded attack. That was at Hounslow Heath in 1786 when the service was in its infancy.

The highwayman who held up a coach as it headed for London was shot dead by the Post Office guard. No-one tried it again.

The mail coaches were not owned by the Post Office but by contractors who also supplied the driver and organised fresh horses at stages along routes. The first coaches were cheaply built but within three years the Post Office had adopted a sturdier design by John Besant, a leading coachbuilder. It lasted some 50 years, until 1836, when the Post Office chose a new design with all the latest features.

The security and speed of the mail coaches made them popular with passengers. Four were allowed inside and later up to three on top, but they would often have to get off and walk up hills to avoid straining the horses.

In the 1830s and early 1840s the nightly departure of the mail coaches from the General Post Office in St Martin's-le-Grand in the City was one of the spectacular sights of London, and on the monarch's birthday a procession of mail coaches from Lin-

Right: The last word in mail-coach design, introduced in 1836. Here the guard is exchanging mail at dawn with a postmaster still in his nightcap.

JUST ARRIVED,

And to be SEEN in a COMMODIOUS BOOTH,

During the Fair,

BALLARD's

GRAND COLLECTION OF

Wild Beasts,

Among which are, THE NOBLE

LIONESS,

FROM AFRICA,

Which attacked the Horse

In the Mail Coach, at Winterslow Hut, near Salisbury, in October last,
But was diverted from its Prey, by a large

MASTIFF DOG.

These Three Animals may now be seen together,
IN PERFECT AMITY!

THE ROYAL

Tiger

Left: With the Birmingham mail coach stuck in snow in 1837, the guard loaded the mail onto the horses and got it through to London. A similar incident in Scotland six years earlier had led to the deaths of the guard and the coachman whose bodies were dug out of deep snowdrifts. The men, James MacGeorge and John Goodfellow, in the highest traditions of the service, had lashed the mail to a post.

Above: Though there is no record of a mail coach being successfully attacked by highwaymen, an attack by a lioness – an escapee from a fair – caused a stir in 1816. The beast's chosen prey, the leading horse, put up a spirited fight and in fact survived, with the help of a mastiff dog that joined in. Subsequently all three were advertised as star fairground attractions.

Far left: The original mail coach that travelled from Bristol and Bath to London in 16 hours in 1784. By Ben Maile.

coln's Inn Fields became a popular tradition, attracting even larger crowds.

But by now the era was drawing to a close. The world's first public railway, between Stockton and Darlington, had opened in 1825, more rail links quickly followed and within five years the first mail was being carried by rail. Passengers, too, were deserting the mail coaches in favour of this exciting steam-powered transport. As the railways spread, the coaches faded away. By 1846 that great nightly exodus from the City had dwindled to a single coach. The last one was from London to Norwich in April of that year.

By then Rowland Hill's uniform penny post and the steam-powered railways were carrying the Royal Mail towards a rapid revolution in the world's postal services.

As the mail coach era draws to a close, the Louth mail coach, horse-drawn to the Lincolnshire town and back as far as Peterborough, is finally – and symbolically – hauled by railway engine on the next stage of its journey back to London. The date: 19 December 1845.

Chapter 3
The Pillar Box

The next famous name to figure in the story of the Royal Mail is Anthony Trollope, the novelist. He was responsible for the first British pillar box. More precisely the first four, sited in St Helier, Jersey, and used from Tuesday, 23 November 1852.

The Post Office already had posting boxes, but these were merely apertures for posting directly into the local letter office, usually in the window pane.

What Anthony Trollope was suggesting was free-standing pillars sited away from post offices, where the public could post letters for collection later. A Post Office official on Jersey at the time, Trollope was making general proposals for improving the postal services on the island. Pillar boxes were not entirely his own idea.

Left: Anthony Trollope, Post Office official, pillar box pioneer and popular novelist.

ROAD-SIDE LETTER BOXES.

Notice to the Public.

On and after the 23rd Nov., Road-side Letter Boxes will be opened for collecting the public corespondence in the following situations :—

DAVID PLACE,
Nearly opposite the Rectory.

NEW STREET,
In front of Mr. Fry's, Painter and Glazier.

CHEAPSIDE,
Top of the Parade.

ST. CLEMENT's ROAD,
Corner of Plaisance.

The Letter Boxes will be cleared daily (Sundays excepted) at the following periods, until further notice :

SIX A. M. AND AT NOON,

Except on Mail-days, when, instead of at Noon, they will be cleared as soon as the Packet is signalled.

Letters deposited in these Boxes will be disposed of in all respects in the same manner as if posted at the Principal Office, previous to the above-named period.

Post-office, St. Helier, November, 1852.

PRINTED AT "THE JERSEY TIMES" OFFICE, LIBRARY-PLACE.

Above: One of the original Channel Islands boxes, first sited on Guernsey, now in Broad Street, Bristol. It has been painted green, the colour of mainland boxes until 1874, though the original Jersey boxes were red.

Left: The poster announcing the first pillar boxes in the United Kingdom, on Jersey in 1852.

He had seen them operating in France. But he was the man who got them started in Britain.

A month after their introduction on Jersey, the postmaster there wrote recommending their use more widely.

Left: Britain's oldest working box at Bishops Caundle, in Dorset. Sited there in 1853, it is based on the original Jersey design, but with a vertical posting aperture.

Right: London's first pillar box, sited in 1855 at the bottom of Fleet Street, just less than half a mile from the General Post Office, near St Paul's. By Ben Maile.

Within three months they had spread as far as Guernsey, where one of Trollope's originals, the hexagonal pillar box in Union Street, survives today. (Another example was brought to the mainland in 1969 and sited in Broad Street, Bristol.)

The first box to appear on the mainland, also in 1853, was at Botchergate, Carlisle. A box of that year still stands at Barnes Cross, Bishops Caundle, in Dorset. It is Britain's oldest working pillar box.

London began to catch up two years later. On Wednesday 11 April 1855, six boxes were opened for posting, sited in Fleet Street, the Strand, Pall Mall, Piccadilly, Grosvenor Place and Rutland Gate (just below Hyde Park). They were big rectangular boxes designed by the Post Office's consulting engineer, A E Cowper. Nobody liked them very much, including Mr Cowper, and before the end of the year he himself was suggesting a change.

The outcome, a design from the

Department of Science and Art, was in marked contrast to Mr Cowper's five-foot-high boxes. They were very ornate and attractive, standing just 4ft high and 1ft 9in wide, and were immediately popular. So much so that, though they were designed for London, they began to appear in other main centres.

Meanwhile, other pillar box designs were taking shape. A Derby firm was making them similar to the originals in the Channel Islands, but with a vertical, not horizontal aperture. In a subsequent version they remembered to add an hours-of-collection plate and the words 'Post Office'.

Another firm made three fluted pillar boxes topped with a high dome and a crown giving them an overall height of eight feet. One was sited at Birmingham's New Street station, another on London Bridge where it served for over 50 years. Modified

The striking eight-foot fluted box of 1856, with its dome and crown, and two modified versions. In all its guises, the box had limited distribution and was a striking exception to the evolution of pillar box design. By Ben Maile.

The attractive, ornate London box of 1857, popular successor to the larger rectangular one.

versions – *sans* dome and crown – continued to be distributed during the following year.

Then another problem emerged. While these slim handsome pillar boxes worked well for London where there were plenty of boxes and frequent collections, they were not big enough for heavy postings in places like Birmingham and Liverpool. Mr Cowper was asked to think again, and again there was a false start.

A large box sited in Liverpool failed

its trial because people could not only post letters, they could get their hand inside and unpost them!

Finally, in 1859, a fresh contract was placed for 100 boxes in two sizes, about 4ft 6in high, with a protective hood above a horizontal aperture. Pillar boxes were beginning to look more like the ones we are familiar with. These were very popular, and the makers were inundated with extra orders.

But not from Liverpool. The postal

Far left: The first standard box for the provinces, based on London's but without the ornate decoration, introduced in 1857.

Centre: The first standard nationwide pattern, introduced in 1859, with distinctive high aperture and protective hood.

Above: Liverpool's 1863 variation on the national theme – larger and with a crown.

powers there decided they needed something bigger. A senior postal official, a Mr Gay, designed one, and was allowed to place it near St George's Hall. It was similar to the popular national design but bigger – and it had a crown on top. Another six similar boxes were duly authorised.

Within months the Post Office had gone off the idea of cylindrical pillar boxes. They should be hexagonal, said the Secretary of the Post Office – and

his Postmaster General agreed. Hexagonal would be more attractive.

J W Penfold, an architect and surveyor, was asked to design it. In October 1865 his designs for hexagonal boxes in three sizes were approved. Construction work was put in hand and the new design was introduced from September 1866.

It lasted for 13 years – but not without another fundamental change. Though the original pillar boxes on Jersey were painted red, the main-

land authorities had chosen dark green. In 1874 they decided that perhaps Anthony Trollope had a point. Dark green was dingy. Red would make the boxes easier to pick out. As a trial, a number of pillar boxes in London were painted red.

They did not need much of a trial. Red was definitely the colour. By July of that year red was adopted as standard for London, and soon afterwards for all pillar boxes. However, the change was to be made only when the boxes needed repainting. The whole process took ten years.

Far Left: The handsome Penfold, which reigned from 1866 to 1879 – and has returned as an optional extra choice from 1989.

Centre: One of the anonymous boxes of 1879 which spread undetected for eight years. Its successor was, basically, today's most familiar design.

Left: The familiar oval, two-aperture London box which has served the capital throughout this century.

Above: Back to a rectangular shape in 1968 – but the sheet steel rusted.

At last, in 1980, a successful 20th century design, but only to complement, not replace, its elderly cousin. With the London oval and the revived Penfold, postmasters now have a choice of four.

And, amid all the repainting, the Post Office decided that, after all, cylindrical, not hexagonal, was the appropriate shape for pillar boxes.

There had been faults in the internal mechanism of the hexagonal boxes. Letters were being caught up and delayed. So in June 1876 the Postmaster General approved the demise of the handsome Penfold and the return of the earlier shape, a design and construction process that took three years.

But the complaints continued. Larger letters and newspapers were liable to get stuck at the top of the new high aperture boxes.

In August 1883 an improved model took to the streets, London's Newgate Street to be precise. It had an aperture just a few inches lower. This did the trick and the following April the new design became standard.

Just one small point had been overlooked. None of the boxes introduced since 1879 had a royal cipher, or indeed any indication that they belonged to the Post Office. It was eight years before that was sorted out. In 1887 yet another new design was approved, this time properly identified.

The contract for London's familiar

oval pillar boxes with two separate compartments was placed as long ago as 1899. In those days they were to separate town and country letters; today they are equally useful for first and second class post.

Another change was on the way in 1912 when the Postmaster General decided that his pillar boxes were unsightly objects. Students of the Royal College of Art were invited to design a new one, incorporating all the improvements agreed over the years. World War One put a stop to that.

There was to be another world war – and a further 20-odd years of peace – before the Post Office decided the time was right for further change. It was to be not cylindrical nor hexagonal but, in line with that very first London box, rectangular. The snag this time was that the sheet-steel welded construction turned out not to be dog-resistant. They corroded.

So they were dropped, and in 1980 came the first successful 20th century design. It is a round modern version of the old familiar pillar boxes, with the same black base but without the 'beret' on top.

But the Post Office has learned a thing or two in its 135 years of pillar box problems. The new box does not replace its more familiar cousin. It takes its place alongside it, ready to be sited at any location where a modern-looking box would be appropriate.

A third choice is the larger two-aperture oval box for London and other centres where two apertures are useful. The modern version has larger doors at the front compared with each end on the earlier ones.

Now a fourth choice has appeared in the Post Office catalogue. In June 1989, more than 120 years after it first appeared on the streets, the six-sided Penfold design was restored to favour.

Exact copies of J W Penfold's original, even bearing Queen Victoria's coat of arms, have been re-cast and are now available for siting in conservation areas, places of historical interest and suitable tourist attractions – in fact, all the best places!

Could it be that the Post Office has at last found the answer to pillar box selection?

Chapter 4
Post Offices

September 1861 is a key date in the development of post offices as we know them. It marked the opening of the Post Office Savings Bank.

Here for the first time was a post office transaction that was not linked in some way with postage and the Royal Mail. It was the breakthrough leading to today's unique network of 21,000 post offices dealing with 150 different transactions for some 25 million customers a week.

Before 1861 there was no convenient way for ordinary people to safeguard their savings. Banks were remote places in more ways than one: 15 counties had no savings banks.

The Post Office had proved its reliability in handling money through dealing with postal revenue and the money order service, which it had run since 1838.

The Post Office Savings Bank was introduced cautiously. In the first year only 700 offices were serving as banks (though there was one in every county!), but within two years there were more than 2,500. It was a great boon to the country because in many areas it was the only bank.

Deposits could be as low as a shilling, and later, to encourage thrift among children and manual workers, small deposits could be made by building up sheets of penny stamps. A sheet of 12 (old) pence was accepted as a shilling in the bank.

This brought further expansion and by the mid-1880s there were 8,000 post offices, 3½ million accounts, and deposits of nearly £50 million. The Post Office had established even more firmly its place in the life and economy of the nation – and post offices

were the key links.

The origins of post offices date back as far as the Royal Mail, to the staging posts commissioned by the monarch to speed his messengers on their way with a fresh horse. After 1635, when Charles I made his Royal Mail available to his subjects, more innkeepers became postmasters along the main routes centred on London. There was a big expansion 85 years later when Ralph Allen linked up those main routes with cross-posts to form a comprehensive postal network, and the next step took another 70-odd years when separate local penny posts began to be set up in many main centres.

By this time – the 1790s – the mail was moving away from inns and to-wards reputable shopkeepers, the forerunners of today's sub-postmasters.

These early offices were often just a room in the postmaster's house, with

Far left: This is how the magazine Punch *greeted the prospect of the Post Office Savings Bank in 1861. "Put by for a frosty day" is the message Mr Punch is giving the worker, in the image of the Prime Minister, Mr Gladstone.*

Left: "St Valentine's Day" is the title of this painting dated about 1820. It shows the interior of an early post office, often just a desk beside a window with a posting aperture.

a window to the street through which letters could be handed in for posting, and incoming letters passed to recipients.

Sometimes the postmaster would arrange to deliver the incoming letters locally for a small extra fee, but this was very much a private enterprise arrangement. Only the bigger centres had their own official letter carriers. The only clues to the fact that the shops were also post offices were the opening in the window and the Post Office notices on display.

Rowland Hill's uniform penny post was the next boost to the post office network. The increased use of the postal service that his reforms brought caused letter offices to spring up in many villages, the start of today's rural network of sub-offices that have become such a cornerstone of rural communities and symbol of the Post Office tradition of service to its customers throughout the country.

The origins of the first Crown post offices – those owned and staffed by the Post Office – date from 1854 when the first purpose-built post offices began to appear in the larger centres. A public room with a counter where customers could be served was a novelty for people used to queuing

outside in all weathers for service at a window. It was also needed to handle the increasing number and complexity of counter transactions.

New services included the registration of letters (from 1841) and the Book Post, something that Rowland Hill had pressed for, offering a cheap-

A busy scene outside an 1830s post office. Note the letter carrier, with stick and pouches, leaning against the doorpost, the little boy beside him peeping into the sealed letter sheet, and the posting aperture above the boy's head.

er postal rate for books, to encourage literacy. Introduced in 1848, it helped subscribers to postal libraries to receive and return books by post, and ensured that these libraries could exist and flourish.

Five years later a similar service for businesses, called the Pattern Post, was introduced. It helped trade by offering a special rate for posting samples, catalogues, price lists, etc.

In 1870, nine years after the start of the Post Office Savings Bank, came another big stride forward – the nationalisation of the private telegraph companies. The telegraphs were put under Post Office control and main post offices throughout the country were linked by electric telegraph. Each one had to be wired into the system and have the receiving and sending equipment installed, a considerable operation. This added telegrams to the list of counter transactions, and the foundations were laid for the development and control of Britain's telecommunications links.

The following year the Post Office began to issue dog licences for the first time. They cost 7s 6d (37½p) and the fee was to remain unchanged until they were abolished in 1988. By then they were costing far more to collect than they were bringing in.

In 1881, postal orders were introduced. There were denominations from a shilling (5p) to £1 with com-mission from a halfpenny to two-pence. In the first three months more than 600,000 were sold, filling the need for a secure way to send small amounts of money. The postal order, introduced to augment the money order, has in fact survived it. Money orders were withdrawn in 1973.

Two years later the launch of the Parcels Post (as it was called then) brought new responsibilities for post offices. Here was another major up-heaval. Every one of the 15,000 offices had to be enlarged or adapted for receiving and storing parcels. Every counter had to have new scales to handle the extra weight, and special cork hand-stamps were needed to cancel the postage stamps.

Post Office Counters more recent expansion into retail stationery has its precedent in 1897 when Ordnance Survey maps began to be sold in upwards of 700 main post offices. The offices kept samples from which they took orders, and the maps were posted from the OS office at either South-ampton or Dublin.

Old-age pensions came next, in 1909. Car licences quickly followed, and in 1912 health and unemploy-ment insurance stamps also went on sale on an agency basis.

In 1915 the Post Office helped to float a war loan scheme, organised through its savings bank, which the following year raised £106 million.

Post offices continued to develop the range of their services – recorded delivery from 1961; philatelic services

The first postal order ever issued.

mushroomed from their introduction in 1963; National Girobank (now Girobank plc, with more than two million current accounts) from 1968; visitors' passports from 1974 – up to today's 150 types of transaction.

In recent years – in common with the Royal Mail and Royal Mail Parcels – Post Office Counters has become a business in its own right within the Post Office Corporation. In an increasingly competitive market, Post Office Counters now has its own management and staff concentrating on the special demands of operating the country's biggest and most important retail chain.

A limited company since October 1987, Counters remains what it has always been, a unique blend of public and private enterprise, with 1500 Crown post offices and 19,500 sub-offices handling transactions mainly on behalf of government departments and other Post Office businesses. The former Post Office Savings Bank, for instance, ceased to be a part of the Post Office in 1969, but Counters continues to handle the business on an agency basis for National Savings.

About half the network is made up of rural offices which together make a loss of between £20 million and £30

This topical promotional photograph shows just a few of the 150 types of transaction on offer in post offices.

The rural post office at St Eval, near Wadebridge, Cornwall. By Ben Maile.

The face of the modern post office – at Basildon, in Essex, one of hundreds of offices Post Office Counters has refurbished since it became a limited company within the Post Office in October 1987.

million a year. The Post Office, with the support of the Government, is committed to maintaining that public service.

On the other hand, if it is to compete successfully in the High Street, it must operate efficiently. To this end it continues to seek to expand the choice of services and products so that more customers are attracted into post offices, keeping staff usefully occupied and making best use of the centrally sited outlets.

It is also overhauling its network, converting some Crown offices to agencies and developing a new part-time contract for the smaller rural offices. This has led to the reopening of some offices that had closed through lack of anyone willing to take them on full time.

Post Office Counters also continues to take steps to cut waiting times at counters. These include taking on more part-time staff at predictable peak periods, introducing express service positions for quick transactions and investing in electronic stamp vending machines that take all coins and give change.

The next counter revolution has already begun. The pilot introduction

Electronic stamp vending machines, giving change for all coins, and phonecard machines are saving customers time at the post office of the 1990s.

of counter automation at 250 offices in the Thames Valley, with computer terminals at counter positions, offers a glimpse of the post offices of the future.

Today's modern post office, with its welcoming decor, its staff in smart matching clothing, the browser units and Postshops displaying and selling a variety of stationery, the electronic vending and the video display, has come a long way from those early letter receiving offices.

It is a success story built on trust, on public confidence that is, happily, taken for granted. Counters' tradition of service to its customers is as strong today as it has ever been.

Universal Postal Union 1874/1974

8ᵖ Airmail blue van and postbox 1930

Chapter 5
The Royal Mail Abroad

The origin of the overseas public postal service pre-dates its inland counterpart. The office of Postmaster General for Foreign Parts was created in 1619 – 16 years before Charles I opened up his Royal Mail for the use of his subjects. Though intended primarily for letters of state it was used by merchants and became more generally available before 1635.

The service had its own couriers with distinctive badges who not only carried letters between London and the continent, they also collected and delivered them in London. There was a public office beside the Royal Exchange in the City of London with writing desks and posters giving details of twice weekly despatches and an express post for urgent items.

Normally the messengers would ride to Dover and travel on the ship to

Falmouth Harbour around 1850. For 200 years Falmouth was Britain's key packet boat station.

Calais or Dunkirk to hand over the mail to the postmaster there.

The early history of the Royal Mail is the story of the packet boats. These were boats that carried mail and whose schedules and ports of call were geared to the needs of that mail.

In those early days many letters were carried privately. Incoming ships' captains were given a penny for every letter they delivered to the postmaster. This would be added to the delivery charge. In the other direction, captains would pick up let-

The sleek lines of the Falmouth packet Marquess of Salisbury, in 1822.

Left: The Cunard steamship Britannia which opened the fortnightly transatlantic mail service on 4 July 1840. The ship is shown leaving Boston on 3 February 1844, en route for Liverpool. Picture courtesy the National Maritime Museum.

Right: The Great Western, heavyweight contender in the Great Transatlantic Sea Race of 1838. By Ben Maile.

ters from labelled bags hung in coffee houses or inns where they met merchants to discuss cargoes.

The system was tightened up in 1799 under the control of a Ship Letter Office. From then on the captains received twopence a letter and the Royal Mail charged fourpence as well as the inland charge from the port to the letter's destination. This charge went up to sixpence then eightpence (in 1815) and remained at this high level long after the inland uniform penny post was established.

The first official packet boats sailed from Dover to France and Flanders, then a packet station was set up in 1660 at Harwich to serve the Netherlands, and nine years later at Falmouth, for Spain and Portugal.

Other stations followed, including Holyhead, Liverpool and Weymouth, but it was Falmouth that was to grow in importance over the next century with new links to the West Indies, to British fleets in the Mediterranean and, by 1800, to America and Canada.

At first there were two vessels at Falmouth, then a third to ensure a fortnightly service to Spain. It was the start of an historic and dramatic period for the Cornish port, covering two centuries. In 1823 there were some 26 Falmouth packets and it was from Falmouth in 1874 that the last packet boat crossed the Atlantic under sail.

That at least was a safe journey. The early transatlantic packet ships – to the West Indies – sailed into waters ruled by pirates. Only three ships completed round trips in that first year (1702), and two of those had narrow escapes.

Later, in the early 1800s, it was not the pirates but the customs men that the packet boat sailors were battling with. Small-time smuggling of tea and tobacco was common practice among the lowly paid seamen, and when the customs swooped on the crew of two Falmouth packets it sparked a mutiny that spread through the Falmouth station.

The ringleaders were imprisoned on one of the warships in the harbour and other crewmen who stormed the packet office in protest – and demanding better wages – were only dispersed after the reading of the Riot Act.

The whole town, heavily dependent on the packet business, was punished. The packet service was removed to Plymouth. But within three months – after the Falmouth people had promised to behave themselves – it was back.

However there was no increase in wages – and probably little decrease in smuggling – and in 1823 the Admiralty took over the Falmouth station and, four years later, all the other packet stations. Control did not return to the Post Office until 1860.

The story of the Royal Mail overseas continues with the development of services across the Atlantic, then to India and finally to Australia and, with the Pacific link, round the world. First they were routes pioneered over land and sea – with the excitement of steam taking over from sail – then, in the 20th century, a new breed of pioneer met the same challenges by air.

Steamship links with America were founded on the Great Transatlantic Sea Race of 1838. The contestants: the heavyweight *Great Western*, 1,340 tons, designed by Brunel for the Great Western Railway to link London with New York, and the 700-ton *Sirius*, representing the British and American Steam Navigation Company.

The *Sirius* set off first, leaving Cork on 4 April. The *Great Western* left Bristol three days later and both ships arrived in New York on the 23rd, the

Sirius, taking 18 days, just hours ahead of its larger rival which made it in 15. New Yorkers turned out to give both ships a great reception.

The achievement also made a deep impression on a certain Samuel Cunard of Nova Scotia. The following year he sailed to England and, with partners from Scotland and Liverpool, won a seven-year mail contract linking Liverpool with Halifax and Boston.

The *Britannia*, one of four Cunard ships built on the Clyde, began the fortnightly service on 4 July 1840, reaching Halifax in just 13 days and Boston a day later.

Challenges to the Cunard supremacy led to the Blue Riband award for the fastest crossing, first won by the Cunard ship *Persia* in 1856. The time: nine days and five hours.

The first Post Office service to India dates from 1815. HMS *Iphigenia* sailed round Africa and reached Calcutta after a five-month voyage. Not a success, but in 1835 they found a route that included an overland trip across Egypt, linking with steamships between Suez and Bombay. This halved the time of the all-sea route round Africa.

In 1839 they added an extra, faster

service by mail coach across France and by ship from Marseilles to Malta where it linked up with the main batch of Indian mail which had travelled by sea from Falmouth.

In 1840 a new contract provided for a through service first to India then on to the Far East. The contractors: the Peninsular and Oriental Steam Navigation Company, better known today as P&O.

The route built up in stages, to Alexandria in 1840, Ceylon, Madras

The P&O steamship Hindostan leaving Southampton on 24 September 1842 carrying mail to India.

and Calcutta in 1843, Penang, Singapore and China in 1845 and Hong Kong in 1848. It was an amazing journey: the mails, unloaded at Alexandria, travelled by steamship through the Mahmoudieh Canal to the Nile, by steamer again down the Nile to Cairo, then by relays of camels and donkeys across the desert from Cairo to Suez from where the P&O

ship carried it eastwards.

At this stage Anthony Trollope, of pillar box fame, reappears. He was the senior postal official whose negotiations in Egypt led to the Royal Mail being carried on the newly completed rail link with Suez. The Suez Canal opened in 1869 but it was not until 1888 that it began to be used regularly for all Indian mail.

The first packet service to Australia in 1844 was a failure. The *Mary Sharpe* took 131 days to reach Sydney. Eight years later P&O stepped in and its small 700-ton, 80 horsepower vessel, the *Chusan*, took just 84 days to reach Sydney and become the first ocean steamer to make the journey.

But the first regular service failed within a year and the Crimean War caused further problems. Instead, in 1855, sailing clippers provided a monthly round-the-world service, going out via the Cape of Good Hope and the Indian Ocean and returning via the Pacific and Cape Horn.

In April 1891 a new route to Japan and China opened up – via the Atlantic and across Canada on the Canadian Pacific Railway. The journey took 28 days compared with 43 via Suez. Six years later the trans-Canada route also began to be used

RAF airmen load a De Havilland DH9 with mail for the British Army of Occupation in Germany just after the end of World War One. These were the first British overseas mail flights.

for Australasian mail.

These had been pioneering days, and they began all over again after World War One, this time by air.

The first barrier, the Channel, was conquered by the RAF in 1918, first with a mail and passenger service to the peace conference in Paris (1020 bags of mail and 744 passengers carried in less than a year) then in December all-mail flights began from

Folkestone to Cologne for the British Army of Occupation. Often the heavily loaded aircraft, to avoid getting bogged down on muddy airstrips, would drop the mail by parachute.

Within a year – on 11 November

1919 – the first regular airmail service began between London and Paris. The Post Office saw this as a trial and added a surcharge of 2s 6d (12½p) an ounce, seeing the airborne letter as something akin to a semi-urgent telegram. Letters had to be enclosed in an outer cover addressed to the Postmaster, Croydon.

But not for long. In the summer of 1920 the fee was cut to twopence (on top of the 2½d ordinary postage) and the Royal Mail introduced a simpler way of getting the letters sorted from the rest of the mail: special blue labels with the words 'By Air Mail', an early idea that has stood the test of time.

Alcock and Brown's historic first transatlantic flight in June 1919 brought 197 letters. Their twin-engined biplane sunk its nose into an Irish bog just 16 hours after take-off from Newfoundland. But the Atlantic remained a formidable barrier to regular airmail flights. The air pioneers made better progress in the other direction.

First, in August 1921, a regular RAF flight from Cairo to Baghdad added a dimension to the routes east

Left: A blue airmail pillar box beside the statue of Sir Rowland Hill outside London's Chief Post Office in 1935.

The Empire Class flying boat helped to pioneer the early mail routes. By Ben Maile

of Suez. By adding 'By air – Cairo-Baghdad' to your envelope you could have your letter taken by P&O to Egypt then flown to Baghdad in a total of ten days compared with 27 without the air link.

The next objective was India. The first step was an Imperial Airways flight from Cairo to Basra on the Persian Gulf. Persia's initial refusal to allow flights over its territory took two years to overcome. The route finally opened with a flight from Croydon on 30 March 1929. This took the mail via Paris to Basle. The next leg, from Basle to Genoa, was by rail, and from Genoa to Alexandria by flying boat. Finally a De Havilland 66 flew the mail over Persia to Karachi. The trip took just over a week.

In 1933 the route was extended to Calcutta then over the Burmese jungle to Rangoon, and by the end of the year it stretched all the way to Singapore. A year later – on 8 December 1934 – came the first regular mail flight from London to Brisbane. A journey of 12,700 miles, it was the longest air route in the world. Various aircraft – land based and flying boats, depending on the terrain – were used on each trip, which took about 12 days.

The other great Empire route, to Africa, had begun on 28 February 1931, with weekly mail and passenger

A blue airmail van unloading at Croydon airport around 1930.

Left: An envelope carried on the first return airmail flight from India (Karachi) to London on 4 April 1929.

flights between London and Tangany-ika (now Tanzania). A regular service to Cape Town started a year later, on 20 January 1932.

Although by the mid-thirties there was still no regular transatlantic air service, the Post Office was making ambitious plans for an Empire air mail scheme. All letters were to go by air, there would be faster schedules, more frequent flights and night flying for the first time. All this for one-and-a-half-pence for half an ounce compared with the same price for one ounce surface rate.

It was a remarkable deal considering that it would now take only two days to India, four to Singapore and seven to Australia.

The scheme, involving extensive use of large flying boats, opened in June 1937 with a service to South Africa. India was added the following February, Australia in July. In its first year the mail doubled to 40 million items and it doubled again in the 12 months to March 1939.

The Atlantic remained the last great barrier. It was not until August 1939 that the large flying boats *Cabot* and *Caribou* inaugurated the British North Atlantic air mail service. There was time for eight round trips before

A streamlined airmail van brings mail to Croydon where the aircraft Horatius, of Imperial Airways, awaits it.

war intervened.

Since the war the Royal Mail's overseas operation has grown out of all recognition. Today, Royal Mail International is a major business, dispatching 540 million items a year, including more than 400 million by air.

Hub of the airmail operation is London's Heathrow Airport, where 81% of all outward airmail is routed by supermarket-style barcode technology through RMI's own modern terminal building, opened in November, 1989. Gatwick, Manchester and Glasgow handle a further 14% between them.

The other 5%? That goes by road! Daily trunkers to Paris, Ostend and

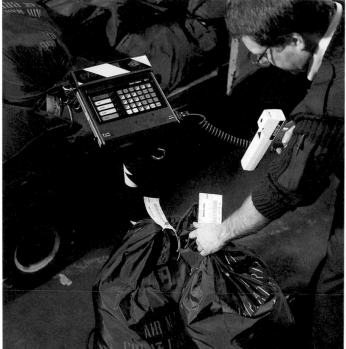

Barcode technology keeps a computerised check on Royal Mail International traffic at Heathrow.

Mail being checked on the conveyor belt in RMI's new Heathrow terminal.

Rotterdam, driven straight on to hovercraft or ferries, carry the mail door to door as fast as it would go by air.

Container lorries also drive on to ferries with printed papers and other lower-priced mail for Spain, Portugal, Italy and most of Scandinavia, as well as France, Belgium and the Netherlands.

This is just a small part of the surface mail worldwide, most of which goes through one of two south-east ports, Tilbury or Felixstowe.

But aircraft are now the main carriers of mail to and from this island. The route to Australasia, for instance, has grown out of all recognition since those early pioneer days. Today there are 42 flights a week to eight Australian airports and seven flights to three New Zealand destinations.

In all, every week Royal Mail International uses 1,400 flights to carry mail direct to 155 countries. And though incoming mail is lighter in terms of overall weight, RMI staff receive a similar number of items, guiding them swiftly into the inland mail network.

RMI also exports British postal expertise through its British Postal Consultancy Service. Many countries worldwide call on the BPCS for help and at any given time there may be a dozen British projects in train, including multi-million pound installations of new postal systems with the machinery, the buildings and the staff training to go with them.

Chapter 6
Postmen in Uniform

It was not until 1872 that all the country's postal delivery force was in uniform. That was the year the Post Office decided that its rural letter carriers should have a uniform, too.

It comprised a military-style blue tunic, fully buttoned down the front with a red stand-up collar. There were winter trousers in blue and summer trousers in grey, each with red piping down the seams.

The move to provide uniforms for everyone on delivery had stemmed from the Post Office take over of the telegraph companies two years earlier. The new boy messengers had to have uniforms, partly because some of the telegraph companies had given their boys uniforms as a supplement to their wages.

This was something the Post Office had not previously thought of, and the issue to rural letter carriers in 1872 was part of the review of wages.

But the true beginning of the postman's uniform goes back a further 100 years to a Post Office in crisis. Not a day went by in the early 1770s without at least one mounted postboy being held up and robbed. The answer, as John Palmer suggested, was the mail coach with a special guard for the mail. The guard would carry pistols and blunderbuss – and he would wear a uniform. To add to the deterrent it would be a military-style uniform which in those days meant that it would be predominantly red. That was in 1784.

This uniform was still being worn 120 years later by one man, Moses James Nobbs. He became a mail coach guard in 1836 and though he transfer-

This remarkable portrait shows the first Post Office uniform – that of the mail coach guard – worn by the last, and most famous of the mail coach guards, Moses James Nobbs.

red to the railways when the mail coach era ended, he refused to wear anything but his old scarlet guard's uniform. He served for 55 years and was still on duty at the Penny Post Jubilee celebrations in 1890.

The mail coach guard became the one Post Office employee on the mail coaches. He was in charge and he was successful. The uniform, of scarlet coat with blue lapels and gold braid, and black hat with gold band, earned respect throughout the land, and that strong scarlet element, though mod-

A District Letter Carrier
1837 ~ 1855

General Post Letter Carrier
1793 ~ 1855

ified over the years, has, with one notable exception, been an integral part of every postman's uniform to this day. It also became the traditional colour for vehicles, pillar boxes and post offices.

London's 'General Post' letter carriers were the next to be issued with uniforms. There were some 230 of them responsible solely for the mail coming into and going out of London. In 1793, nine years after the introduction of the uniformed mail coach

guard, these London men were given a similar outfit: scarlet cutaway coat with blue lapels and cuffs, brass buttons with the wearer's number, and a beaver hat with gold band and cockade.

They were introduced despite opposition from the Secretary of the Post Office. He argued that a uniform would not deter someone determined to commit a 'bad action' and though it 'may prevent loitering and mis-spending their time in ale houses or disorderly places' the good would not

Letter Carrier 1855 ~ 1860.

equal the expense of clothing such a large number of people. He estimated the cost would 'exceed £600 a year'.

The men were not happy either. They had to be convinced that there was no reflection on their honesty and that wearing a uniform would not mark them out as a target for robbery.

Not much happened over the next 40 years, except that the uniform began to be introduced in other large centres, starting with Edinburgh and Dublin. Then in 1837, the carriers of London's locally posted letters – the

Letter Carrier, 1861

POSTMAN, 1936

'tuppenny postmen' – were given a uniform. They had a similar beaver hat but instead of the scarlet coat theirs was blue with a scarlet collar.

This then was the position when Rowland Hill brought in his 1840 penny post reforms: the General Post men in red coats, and the London Post men in blue, both making deliveries in London, but with the men in blue more in evidence on the streets.

Up to now the significant item missing from the uniforms was trous-

Opposite page, far left: Echoes of the mail coach guard's military outfit.

Centre: The "Tuppenny postmen" got their uniforms in 1837, 44 years after their General Post brethren.

Right: In 1855 the two London units combined into this eye-catching ensemble, with trousers issued for the first time. The original beaver hat was soon replaced by this tall shiny one.

This page, left: The more practical blue uniform – but retaining the red trimmings – introduced in 1861. In 1868, a military-style tunic replaced the frock-coat and waistcoat. This was the first truly nationwide uniform.

Centre: The postman of the 1930s. The peaked cap dates from 1932.

Below: The grey uniform, introduced in 1969.

ers. Letter carriers had to supply their own and many were in marked contrast to their grand coats and beaver hats, to the delight of humorists and cartoonists of the period.

The London postmen got their trousers in 1855 and at the same time the two London postal units – the General Post and the London Post – were combined and given one standard uniform. The design chosen for the new London District letter carriers was more akin to the less familiar General Post carriers than to the blue-coated London Post men. It was an eye-catching scarlet frock-coat with smart grey trousers.

When the formerly baggy-trousered letter carriers appeared on the streets in their new garb there was considerable comment in the press, and *Punch*, in an article headed 'The Post Office in a Blaze', voiced mock concern about the danger of flirtations with captivated female servants delaying the Royal Mail. The *Illustrated Glasgow News* declared itself 'astonished at the liberality of the Government' in supplying so brilliant and complete an ensemble.

Waterproof capes were also introduced at this time, protecting both the mail and its carrier, and the beaver

hat was replaced by a tall hard shiny hat as worn by letter carriers in Paris. While the cape was here to stay, the hat lasted only four years. A hard felt hat followed which in turn gave way to the single peaked shako.

From 1855 the extension of the uniform to the provinces was gradual and, initially at least, trouserless. In 1856 uniforms were extended to towns where there were 13 or more letter carriers, but the senior postal official in Manchester pressed for a lower limit, stressing the importance of anyone seen opening one of the new pillar boxes being recognised as a Post Office servant.

By 1859 the limit had been reduced to four and the following year a uniform was given to all letter carriers in post offices where there was a scale of wages proper to them. But this still excluded the rural men and the battle was still on for provincial trousers.

The postmaster of Liverpool joined the fray: 'So long as the men have to furnish themselves with trousers they will wear articles so shabby as to be a discredit to the service...'

But the trouser split was overshadowed the following year – 1861 – by the demise of the scarlet coat. The

Post Office had discovered what any housewife could have told them: that scarlet was not a practical working colour. Navy blue became the choice for frock-coat, waistcoat and trousers, the frock-coat and waistcoat being replaced seven years later by the military-style tunic that, with trousers, became the first to be worn by

Above: This double-peaked shako, introduced in 1896, kept the rain off London postmen's necks until the peaked cap was introduced in 1932.

This felt hat replaced the old straw boater in 1929. The photograph was taken in the Isles of Scilly, in 1936.

Left: Straw-hatted postwomen at Barnet during World War One.

letter carriers throughout the country.

Though London and Edinburgh had their own ideas for a time, adopting a tunic with tails (for warmth plus ease of climbing stairs) the military tunic remained the standard winter garb until 1910, when the existing summer style, a lounge-suit jacket, was adopted year-round.

London postmen had also been given a new hat in 1896, a double-peaked shako replacing the single peak.

By 1910 the uniform and protective clothing scene had become so involved that a committee was appointed to sort it out. Sort it out it did, cutting the numbers of patterns of the various garments from 92 to 56. They were in six classes: supervisors got the superior version; then doorkeepers, etc; postmen and postwomen were in the third class, followed by porters, liftmen, etc, then mail-cart drivers and finally boy messengers.

The committee also dealt with conditions for issuing protective clothing, and how long each garment was expected to last. It also introduced knickerbockers and puttees for postmen and boy messengers on cycling duties, but after 15 years they were discarded at the request of the staff.

In World War One, as the men left to join the forces, thousands of women took over the postal deliveries, and their uniforms of navy blue serge tunics and skirts and blue straw hats were strongly in evidence. The war also brought a shortage of postal uniforms (the armed forces had priority) and there were bonuses for extended wear.

The postwomen's straw hats lasted until 1929 when a more fashionable blue felt hat in the Girl Guide style found favour. Postmen's headgear changed three years later, a peaked cap taking over from the shako.

A spurt of changes in the fifties

The uniform of today: a return to the familiar navy blue, and with shirt and tie to complete the outfit. Postwomen have a beret and a choice of trousers or skirt.

began with a new summer uniform in 1955, a switch from single to double-breasted jacket the following year and new cap and uniform badges in 1958.

The switch from navy blue to grey in 1969 was the next big change. Grey trousers were not new – they were first issued with the scarlet frock-coat that so dazzled the populace of the late 1850s – but an all-grey outfit was quite a departure.

It lasted just 15 years to 1984 when

trials of a more modern version of the traditional navy-blue led to its restoration, along with the traditional red trimming. This time the ensemble included shirt and tie.

The scarlet of that original frock-coat was back and, in today's postman's wardrobe – particularly the weather-proof jacket and the delivery pouch – the traditional Post Office red is more prominent than at any stage since those proud frock-coat days.

Chapter 7
Parcels by post

Two new postal terms entered the language in 1883. The first, Parcels Post, spawned the second. With parcels to deliver as well as letters the term letter carrier had to go. They became postmen.

Parcels Post, as it was then called, was born to competition. Indeed, its birth was delayed for the best part of half a century because of opposition from existing parcel carriers, including the railways.

There were signs of this opposition as early as 1680 when the London merchant William Dockwra set up his London penny post as a private venture. The penny service included parcels weighing up to a pound. It was closed down after two years, then relaunched as part of the Post Office, which continued to carry the parcels for over 100 years. Then, in 1794, the

service was restricted to letters.

It was a restriction that took some shaking off. In the late 1830s, first the postal reformer Henry Cole, then Rowland Hill himself, urged the introduction of a Post Office uniform parcel post. The Book Post, in 1848, and the Pattern Post five years later (see Chapter 4) stemmed from this pressure.

Finally it was developments outside Britain that forced the issue. In 1880, the countries forming the Universal Postal Union agreed to set up an international parcels service. This meant that Britain, a leading member of the UPU, had to operate a parcels service too.

This was the lever needed to over-

Left: The Illustrated London News of 11 August 1883 greeted the birth of the Parcels Post with this front page cartoon.

Henry Fawcett, the blind Postmaster General who negotiated the introduction of the Parcels Post.

come the opposition of the private carriers. The Postmaster General of that time, Henry Fawcett, made full use of it. Though blinded in a shooting accident in his youth, Henry Fawcett had carved out a successful political career and, as PMG under Mr Gladstone, set out to make the Post Office more generally useful to the public.

The creation of the Parcels Post – including the difficult negotiations with the railway companies – was his considerable achievement. Winning

that argument was the first part. He was then faced with the formidable task of introducing the service nation-wide.

It would serve every city and every hamlet. Some 15,000 post offices had to be enlarged or adapted for sorting parcels; every counter had to have the heavier scales to weigh them and new cork handstamps to cancel the postage. Every letter carrier's (now post-man's) walk had to be altered so that the loads were not too heavy.

Special Parcels Post handcarts were introduced; cycles of various designs, with large baskets, began to appear. The Post Office bought hundreds of large wicker baskets to carry the bulk

parcels over the trunk routes between towns. And to carry them by road – it was cheaper than rail – many new Parcels Post van and cart services were planned and set up, with new vehicles specially designed to take the extra weight.

The maximum weight of a parcel was fixed at 7lb, then raised to 11lb three years later. Postage was three-pence for 1lb, sixpence for 2lb, a shilling (5p) for up to 7lb, then 1s 6d (7½p) for 11lb.

Though the Post Office drew the line at carrying 'gunpowder, lucifer matches, bladders containing liquid, live animals and grossly offensive matter' this still left plenty of scope.

The London/Colchester parcel mail coach battling through the snow around 1901.

Top left: One of the earliest of an assortment of pedal-powered vehicles introduced to carry the early parcels. There was also the hen and chickens, featured in Chapter 8.

Left: These parcel handcarts – wicker baskets on wheels – were a useful aid for heavy loads over short distances.

Above: The return of the mail coach, this time for parcels only. Note the guard with his revolver and sword.

The newly named postmen found themselves saddled with game, rabbits and fish along with their letters.

It was the high cost of carrying parcels by rail that led to the return, after an absence of some 40 years, of the mail coach. Like their predecessors, these were specially designed coaches, operated under contract, with one Post Office employee on board to guard the mail. Unlike their predecessors, they carried no passengers, travelling only at night. The guard was armed with a sword and revolver, and also carried a posthorn, but his main task was to sort the parcels.

The coach routes were centred on London, and the first journey in 1887 was to Brighton. By 1895 there were parcel mail coach services to Oxford, Chatham, Colchester, Watford, Windsor, Tunbridge Wells, Bedford and Guildford.

The end of the horse-drawn parcel coach was foreshadowed just 18 years and a day after the London/Brighton parcel coach had begun the second mail-coach age. On 2 June 1905 the first motor-driven coach took over that same London/Brighton route. It was a specially designed coach built on a London bus chassis. The guard

Left: A Scottish version of the parcel mail coach, pictured in Edinburgh around 1900.

Below: The motorised coach that signalled the end of the horse-drawn variety, pictured around 1906.

dispensed with his revolver and sword, substituting a truncheon and police whistle.

But World War One brought a cut-back in motor services and the railways began to take over. By 1920 little over 5% of parcels were travelling any distance by road, and this situation was formalised in 1922 in a deal committing the Post Office to sending no more than 10% of parcels by road.

The Parcels service was only four years old when, in 1887, the Post Office acquired London's most famous sorting office, Mount Pleasant. The building had been a jail and, until 1885, a debtors' prison. Now it was to be a key centre for sorting Post Office parcels. Though new structures were erected on the site, it was not until 1929 that the last of the prison buildings disappeared.

The first part of the present sorting office was completed in 1926 and an extension was opened on 2 November 1934 by the Duke and Duchess of York, later George VI and Queen Elizabeth.

Mount Pleasant had become a key centre for letters as well as parcels, and the Parcel Post continued to be run mainly alongside the Letter Post

This is the House of Correction, Coldbath Fields, North London, as featured in the Illustrated Times in 1867. Later it became a jail, then a debtors' prison. Later still, in 1887, it became a postal sorting office renamed Mount Pleasant. Some prison buildings survived until 1929.

Right: The Duke and Duchess of York touring Mount Pleasant after the Duke had opened the new extension in 1934. The office was described at the time as the biggest sorting office in the world, handling both letters and parcels.

Parcels by motorcycle. The year: around 1932 when the peaked cap began to replace the shako.

Right: The basket carrier tricycle was still earning its keep in the mid-1930s.

with parcel sorting scattered among 1,500 offices. Postmen's muscle was the main motive power, and the Post Office began to look for ways to ease the burden and speed the service.

On 5 December 1967 Postmaster-General Edward Short heralded two important developments in parcel handling: the introduction of containers and the dawn of mechanised

sorting.

The first was comparatively simple. Wheeled containers were already being used to move parcels in London and other major centres. They were carried on vans fitted with powered tail hoists. Containers also began to be used on trains.

The second was more difficult – and more revolutionary. Machines to sort the various shapes and sizes of parcel were complex, bulky and expensive. If parcel sorting was to be mechanised it would have to be concentrated on fewer centres to make the best use of the costly equipment.

The Post Office decided to build 31 highly mechanised parcel concentration offices, each serving a large surrounding area. This was the Parcels service's first significant move away from the letters operation. The second came in 1986 when Royal Mail Parcels was established as a separate business within the Post Office.

It was an important change. Instead of being managed, along with Letters and Counters, by a head postmaster responsible in turn to a regional director, the new Parcels business organised its 31 parcel concentration offices into 12 parcels' districts each with a manager re-

Left: Early tilted-belt parcel sorting machinery at Worcester in 1964.

sponsible to the managing director.

Datapost, the courier service set up in 1970, also became part of the Parcels' business with five districts each led by a manager directly responsible to the centre.

In 1986, Parcels also began to develop a completely separate computer-controlled distribution network, offering business customers 24-hour and 48-hour delivery. Business grew rapidly, and the network grew with it. In two years there were 86 offices grouped into five districts.

The 1986-87 financial year saw the

The central control room at Glasgow parcel concentration office, which opened in June 1983.

business record its strongest growth for a number of years and make record profits against increasingly fierce competition. Independent research confirmed Inland Datapost as the most reliable service of its kind, and its overseas network had expanded to include more than 90 countries.

The overseas parcels service has seen a gradual swing from surface to air transport throughout the 1970s and 1980s. In 1972-73, 60% of overseas parcels went by ship, 40% by air. In 1987-88, 80% of the four million overseas parcels went by air against only 20% by sea. Inward the difference is not so marked: 52/48 in favour of air.

The London Overseas Mails Office handles 96% of all overseas mail travelling by air. Liverpool copes with the bulk of the surface mail, though LOMO deals with 30% of that too.

Inland in 1986, there was another

Left: A Datapost road/air interchange at Manchester. There are nightly Datapost flights linking 12 centres throughout the country.

Far left: A round-the-clock nationwide breakdown service, with central control of 300 repair depots gets vehicles on the move again within 90 minutes.

Top right: A trunker with the new name, adding force to Royal Mail Parcels' image.

switch of transport – from rail back to road. By the year-end, 80 per cent of parcels were being carried by the business's own fleet, and containers were no longer used. A progressive streamlining of the parcel concentration office network followed, and by 1989 the number of offices had been reduced to 24, with further streamlining planned for the early 1990s

A computerised breakdown service, linking 300 motor repair depots with a central 24-hour help line added reliability to the increased flexibility and speed of the road-based networks.

In the summer of 1989 Parcels took another step towards autonomy, announcing plans to move away from the 3,000 sorting offices it shares with the letters business for delivery. Instead, Parcels is establishing some

150 local parcel depots and similar units in satellite buildings grouped round (and sometimes within) the parcel concentration offices. Royal Mail Letters will be sub-contracted to deliver parcels in outlying areas. To match this new independence the business also acquired a new name, Parcelforce, and a new headquarters at Milton Keynes.

The late 1980s and early 1990s will be seen by future postal historians as a dramatic phase for the Post Office parcels operation. But the technology-based Parcels business of the 1990s remains true to the Rowland Hill tradition. It still takes pride in being the only carrier to deliver ordinary parcels, at a uniform price, to any address in the land, no matter how remote.

Chapter 8
By Air, by Land, by Sea, by Hand . . .

The Parcels Post brought a big increase in the volume and weight of inland mail. The postman needed all the help he could get. Carts began to appear, some to push, others to pull. Cycles of two, three, even five wheels were introduced.

Two tricycle posts were established in Coventry as early as 1880, when pedal cycles were in their infancy. Three years later, a Horsham architect invented the five-wheeled centre-cycle, or hen and chickens, as it became known. With the large (hen) wheel supplying the pedalled propulsion, and the four small wheels the balance, this delightful contraption worked quite well.

Within a decade bicycles and tricycles were in use on a number of rural services and in 1896 the Post Office bought 100 more. There was another

big increase the following year when, to mark Queen Victoria's diamond jubilee, delivery rights were for the

first time extended to every household in the land. Until then people in the more remote areas had to pick up their mail from their nearest post office.

In the meantime other imaginative forms of transport were emerging. A Scottish postman, Andrew Lawson, built a steam-driven mail cart, known locally as the Craigievar Express, after his home village in Aberdeen-

Left: The delightful penny farthing, on delivery duty around 1900.

Top right: The "hen and chickens" in line astern at Horsham in the 1880s.

Far right: This tricycle was used between Malpas, in Cheshire, and nearby Barton early this century.

Below right: Postie Andrew Lawson with the "Craigievar Express" he built outside his home.

Far right: An early Daimler van on Royal Mail duty in 1899.

shire. It sped the mail to the nearby village of Whitehouse.

The Post Office was experimenting, too. Early adventures included the use of an electric mail van between the General Post Office, in the City of London, and Paddington sorting office. An oil motor van had a brief trial, carrying mail between the GPO and the south-west London sorting office, and there were similar local experiments with all kinds of vehicles up and down the country.

But in the late 1890s it was still the horse-drawn parcel coach service that carried a significant quantity of mail. Often the horses were hard-pressed to haul it, particularly on the original London to Brighton run. In 1897 a steam-driven mail van service was tried out for six weeks between London and Redhill, the first part of the Brighton journey. It was a useful help – though the horses were marginally faster!

By the turn of the century the motor vehicle was finally out-pacing its four-footed rival: that early steam journey to Redhill was entrusted to internal combustion, though horses still ruled from Redhill to Brighton.

In Manchester, meanwhile, there were motorised links with Liverpool

This early basket-towing moped brightened the roads around Sittingbourne, Kent, in 1902.

Right: Motorised tricycle used on rural delivery around 1905.

Above: Bicycle post on parade at Ellesmere, Shropshire, around 1910.

Left: A little piece of local history at Shenley, in Hertfordshire, around 1912, as the bicycle takes over from the horse and trap. The shelter in the background was one of a number built for country postmen to sort out their mail and keep warm in rough weather.

(36 miles) and Altrincham (nine). A motor-tricycle carrier was being tested in London and by 1903 new motor van services were operating between London and Epping (20 miles), Sunderland and Newcastle (12), Birmingham and Warwick (21) and in parts of central London.

Within two years the horse-drawn parcel coaches were being replaced by motor transport – a specially designed coach built on a London bus chassis. By 1910 there were nearly 70 motor mail services and by 1913 that figure had doubled. The internal combustion engine was on its way.

On 9 September 1911, mail took to the air – from Hendon, Middlesex, to Windsor, in Berkshire, the world's introduction to scheduled airmail flight. It was the first of a planned week-long series of flights to celebrate the Coronation of George V.

Cards and envelopes, specially designed for the flights, could be addressed to anywhere in the country. After the flight they went into the normal post. Such was the demand that the flights had to continue to 26 September to clear the backlog.

But the public's enthusiasm was not shared by the Post Office. The aeroplane of 1911 was too dependent

The scene at Hendon in September 1911, the world's first scheduled air mail flight.

on the weather to be of use on a regular service. For the time being at least, the Royal Mail would concentrate on road-based motor transport. At first it continued to use contractors' vehicles, as it had since the early mail coach days, but after the war it began to build up its own fleet.

The Royal Mail bought a few motor vans in 1919, 50 more in 1920 and 100 in 1921. Within five years the postal fleet – including motor cycles, some with side-cars – was covering some 11 million miles a year. Eight years later, in 1932, there were some 4,000 vehicles, and that figure doubled over the next eight years.

Though mail was still carried on horseback in a few remote areas (even London had a horse-drawn mail van as late as 1949), by the end of the 1930s motorised horsepower had taken over from the four-footed kind.

Britain also had an inland airmail network. Known as the town-to-town service, it opened on 20 August 1934,

Above: The Royal Mail motorised fleet began to take shape after World War One. This was 1919. The Post Office was buying in vehicles, which is why none of them had the Royal Mail livery.

Right: A typical Royal Mail van of the 1930s at Drymen, Glasgow.

serving London, Birmingham, Manchester, Liverpool, Cardiff, Plymouth, Bristol, Southampton, Belfast, the Isle of Wight (Cowes) and the Isle of Man (Douglas).

The service was initially experimental and restricted to mail to and from the listed centres. Airmail stickers were needed, but postcards went for a penny, letters up to two ounces for 1½d. The service lasted until the war.

World War Two transformed aerial transport. The Post Office was not slow to make use of the increasing number of scheduled inland flights to speed first class mail, and by the mid-sixties it was chartering its own aircraft.

The air link between London and Edinburgh has long been a key element in the inland mail network. In what is known today as the night mail jet operation, every week-night at 11.15pm Boeing 757s take off simultaneously from the two capitals, crossing in mid-air.

This is just one link in a complex network of mail routes by road, rail, air and sea. Royal Mail's fleet comprises some 32,000 vehicles. On the railway, 200 trains a night are chartered from British Rail, including 35

travelling post offices. This is in addition to all the mail that travels by the scheduled passenger trains.

In the air each week-night 30 chartered aircraft make a total of 70 flights exclusively for the Royal Mail. Again, this is quite apart from all the mail that has its regular place on scheduled passenger flights, including 66 in Scotland alone, serving the Hebrides and other islands.

By sea, the Royal Mail charters two nightly hovercraft flights from the Isle of Wight to Portsmouth, and there are regular sailings to Belfast from Liverpool and Heysham, and to Liverpool from Belfast and Larne. These are for second class mail: first class goes by air.

The present network, with its increasing use of chartered aircraft, was established on 2 July 1979 when Liverpool's Speke airport became the hub of nightly flights to and from five other provincial centres – the first 'spokes of Speke.'

The operation began as a straightforward aircraft to aircraft transfer,

Above left: Horsham again, 50 years on: from hens and chickens to motorcycles and vans.

Left: The town-to-town inland airmail interchange at Liverpool in the mid-1930s.

involving some 600 mail bags a night, the aircraft returning with mail for their part of the country. Within a decade the operation grew tenfold.

Speke now has 14 'spokes' – Aberdeen, Belfast, Bournemouth, Bristol, Cardiff, Derby, Edinburgh, Exeter, Gatwick, Glasgow, Newcastle, Norwich, Southend and Stansted – and 6,000 bags a night are exchanged in 90 minutes of bustling activity between midnight ·and 1.30am. The operation also involves the use of Royal Mail vans from Chester, Crewe, Leeds/Bradford, Preston, Warrington and Manchester, as well as Liverpool.

In October 1982 a second air hub was created at the East Midlands Airport, 12 miles from Derby. Unlike Speke, with its road/air interchange, Derby's primary role is to link air and rail, though vans are also involved.

The airport bursts into life at 10.30pm, when the first of 13 flights from Scotland, Belfast, East Anglia and south and south-west England arrives. On a normal weekday all 13 have arrived within 40 minutes. Some of them are unloaded, reloaded and flown out again within an hour. Others wait for mail brought in by rail to Derby, midlands hub of the travelling post office network.

A mail exchange in the 1980s on the beach of the Hebridean Isle of Barra, one of 66 flights to Scottish islands.

It is a high-speed exchange with vans rushing mail between the air and rail hubs and carrying it by road to Leicester, Nottingham, Peterborough and Doncaster.

Some 4,000 bags of mail are interchanged nightly at Derby. These, plus the 6,000 at Speke, the 2,500 jetted nightly between London and Edinburgh and the 1,000 or more carried on scheduled passenger flights, amount to some one in eight of all first class mail, an impressive figure considering the high proportion delivered locally.

Hovercraft are used regularly for Isle of Wight mail.

Right: At high tide a rowing boat is pressed into Royal Mail service by associate-postman Len Richie for delivery to families on St Michael's Mount, near Penzance, Cornwall, in 1989.

Ben Maile's painting of the nightly bustle of activity at the East Midlands Airport, Derby.

Some 65 per cent of all mail goes by rail at some point on its journey and almost all of it has a road trip. The travelling post offices, the postbuses and the London underground Mail Rail – each the subject of a separate chapter in this book – all play their part in a complex organisation that grew from the relays of 17th-century mounted postboys, through the cross-posts created by Ralph Allen in the 18th century and the local penny posts pulled together by Rowland Hill's reforms 150 years ago.

In 1840, 68 million Penny Black stamps were sold to cover ten months' postage. It seemed a lot. Yet the Royal Mail of the 1970s was carrying more than 100 times as much mail, and an incredible 40 per cent growth over the decade up to 1989 has brought the volume of letters up to 150 times the 1840 figure. Visionary though he was, even Rowland Hill could hardly have imagined what his postal reform would bring 150 years on.

Personnel carriers in London 160 years apart. Postmen of the 1830s could hop off this vehicle – known as an accelerator – to start their deliveries. The 1990s version (below) has to stop.

Mail Rail

Chapter 9
The Mail Goes Underground

On 3 December 1927 Mrs Thomas Gardiner, wife of the Controller of the London postal service (later Sir Thomas, Post Office Director-General), pulled a lever some 75 feet below Paddington station to send the first cargo of mail on the Post Office's own London underground railway.

It was the climax of a scheme that can be traced back to Rowland Hill. And it was the start of a mail-carrying system that continues to serve the Royal Mail with remarkable efficiency to this day.

Mail Rail, as it is now called, runs for six miles through nine-foot diameter tubes between the Eastern district sorting office at Whitechapel to

The first despatch of mail through the pneumatic tube from the Post Office's North Western district office to Euston, 600 yards to the east, in February 1863.

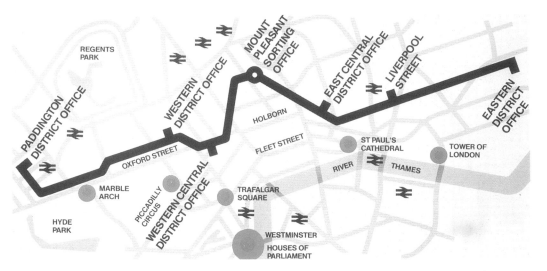

Map showing the Mail Rail route beneath London's busy streets.

Paddington station, via Liverpool Street station, the East Central sorting office in the City (beside the old GPO), Mount Pleasant, West Central and Western district offices, picking up and dropping off mail on its journey.

Today, the 440-volt electric trains run at up to four-minute intervals, 22 hours a day, carrying some 50,000 bags of mail at 35 miles an hour, unhampered by the dense traffic on the streets above. Some 250 staff work exclusively on Mail Rail, and not one of them is a driver. The trains are remotely controlled from switch-frames at each station with a main depot Mount Pleasant.

Rowland Hill's involvement began in the 1850s. Even then there was enough mail to transport across London and enough traffic to hamper its progress to prompt the Penny Post pioneer to propose an underground route. In June 1855, as Secretary of the Post Office, he submitted a report by two eminent engineers on the practicality of a tube running from the General Post Office in the City westwards to Holborn.

Hill's original vision had been even more ambitious. He foresaw 15-inch diameter tubes stretching as far as Dover and Crewe which could 'keep the line of ordinary roads, pass through the heart of towns' and be carried 'through the very post offices along the route.'

But the Post Office role was as an interested observer and what began to emerge was a private enterprise plan for larger pneumatic tubes below London with wheeled vehicles propelled along rails. A stationary steam engine would drive a large fan which could either suck air out of the tube, creating a vacuum and drawing the train towards it, or blow air in to push the train along.

The Pneumatic Despatch Company was formed to pursue the enterprise, and a tube was built which ran for 600 yards from the Post Office's North Western district sorting office eastwards to Euston station. Wrought-iron trucks to carry the mail were 8ft long, just over 2ft wide and ran on a 2ft gauge track.

Experimental trips began in January 1863. Sir Rowland, with his Postmaster-General, Lord Stanley of Alderney, inspected the system and a month later, on 20 February, regular mail-carrying began. There were 30 trains a day, each journey taking little more than a minute. The corresponding horse-drawn van service was discontinued.

Flushed with success, the company began to extend the line eastwards from Euston to Holborn, within a mile of the GPO in the City. This opened two years later. There was just one snag. The Post Office had made no promises that it would make use of it and indeed did not do so. In fact a year later the original, shorter link ceased to carry mail.

Undaunted by this and other problems, the company pressed on, finally completing the link to the GPO. The Post Office was still lukewarm about the enterprise but was persuaded to give it a try. The trip between Euston

and Holborn, including handling at each end, was timed at 17 minutes. As this was only four minutes faster than the horse-drawn vans, the Post Office lost interest again.

This was the end of London's pneumatic tubes and the company was finally wound up by the Board of Trade. The terminus of the tube at the GPO was used to store coal and wood. The pneumatic tunnels would play no part in any future subterranean transmission of mail.

But a start had been made, and the case for an underground system would grow stronger as mail volumes

The control panel at Mount Pleasant in 1935.

Left: The Post Office railway in 1931. These wooden containers were loaded with mail bags then the containers slotted into the carriages of the train. The same system is still used today.

and London traffic increased. The pneumatic pioneers had shown how driverless wagons could be operated over distances below London.

So there was experience to draw on when in 1909 a committee was set up to consider the relative merits of pneumatic tubes and underground electric railways. The committee recommended an underground electric railway, very much along the lines we have today, and plans were put to the Cabinet in November 1912.

Though it was predicted that the line would make a small loss, the Cabinet accepted the Postmaster-General's case that the project was still worthwhile because it would speed the mail, reduce traffic in the streets and noise at night, and reduce dependence on contract labour.

The growing use of motor vehicles was another factor – about one in ten Post Office vans was motorized – and, though they could do 20 miles an hour, 5–8 mph was nearer the mark in London traffic, mainly because of the horse-drawn traffic blocking the streets. As motor transport developed, the traffic speeded up and it is possible that, had the decision on the railway been delayed a few years, it might not have been built.

The impetus generated before the war caused tunnelling to continue after the outbreak. A Treasury suggestion that the work be postponed was rejected in 1916 by Prime Minister Asquith, who said it would endanger work already done and greatly increase final costs.

So by 1917 the tunnels were completed, but, as labour and materials were now scarce, further work was suspended and two people were employed to patrol the tunnel and deal with any minor repairs.

But the tunnels did come in useful in another role: to store treasures safe from Zeppelin raids. From January 1918 a large proportion of the collections of the Tate Gallery and the National Portrait Gallery and material from the Public Record Office were stored in the tunnel at the General Post Office; West Central District Office stored treasures from the British Museum, while Paddington held some of King George V's pictures and the Wallace Collection.

Work on the railway resumed in 1924, first on the 2ft gauge track, then on the lifts, conveyors and chutes, then the rolling stock and signalling.

In 1925, a Mr Evan Evans, on loan from the London Underground Railway, was appointed the first General Manager, and some early rolling stock was delivered.

The 1926 General Strike caused some further delay, but finally engineering tests and staff training began, alternating on various sections of the line. On 4 July 1927 Post Office staff controlled empty trains over the whole system for the first time.

By September the main cabling work was done and by mid-October the final track circuits were ready. At the end of November, a scheduled service of empty trains ran for a week between Paddington and GPO Headquarters (East Central district office). At last – and in time for the Christmas postings – all was ready for that modest but historic opening ceremony by Mrs Gardiner.

Normal services, carrying parcels, began on 5 December between Paddington and Mount Pleasant. The section between Mount Pleasant and Liverpool Street was used during the week before Christmas, and the final link, from Liverpool Street to Eastern District sorting office at Whitechapel, opened for business on 2 January 1928. From this date the trains ran for 21 hours a day – from 10am to 7am – and the corresponding parcel van services were halted from 30 January. The railway carried its first letter traffic two weeks later and this built up over the next few months.

The railway had its share of teething troubles. Inconsistent braking caused some minor collisions and, more seriously, it was found that the curves were too sharp for the four-wheeled cars. A new design of car, with bogies, introduced in 1930, solved the problem.

The railway received its first royal visitor in 1929 – the Prince of Wales, later Edward VIII. Queen Elizabeth the Queen Mother (then Duchess of York) followed in 1932, and Queen Mary and Princess Elizabeth (the present Queen) in 1939.

During the war the tunnels were used by staff as air raid shelters, and though the railway had its share of bomb damage, it kept operating remarkably well. Each morning through the blitz the tunnels were patrolled to check the effects of the previous night's raid. The worst incident was a direct hit on the Parcels block at Mount Pleasant when two railway staff were killed.

The railway has been filmed and featured on radio a number of times, including a broadcast by Brian Johnston in December 1954 when he travelled as a posted packet in a railway container.

A special postmark and an exhibi-

Crossed union jacks for the anniversary train. Half a century of carrying mail under London's traffic-choked streets is celebrated as Mr Dennis Roberts, Managing Director of Posts in 1977, presses a button to start the golden jubilee journey from the East Central sorting office near St Paul's.

tion at King Edward Building, the East Central office, marked the railway's 40th birthday in 1967. The Postmaster-General, Mr Edward Short, and a party of journalists travelled on a special train from Mount Pleasant to East Central for the opening. There was a similar exhibition for the 50th anniversary.

The electric trains used today, of which there are 34, were built by Greenbat, a Leeds company specialising in the construction of mining locomotives, and were introduced in 1979. They are of the same basic dimensions as the original trains which they were intended to replace, but such has been the growth in traffic in recent years that several of the original trains have been brought out of retirement, rebuilt and returned to service.

In 1987, to celebrate the Diamond Jubilee of the Railway, the POR was re-christened 'Mail Rail', three of the new trains were rebuilt with streamlined casings and a new record of 12 minutes set up for the non-stop run from Liverpool Street to Paddington.

Left: Activity on Mail Rail below London's busy streets. By Ben Maile.

Right: Mail Rail loading, 1990s style, showing one of the latest trains.

The streamlined casings have proved to have a practical effect, too, making the trains easier to keep clean and maintain.

Though the early decision to build the railway was based on comparison with horse-drawn traffic, that decision is just as valid today. With the volume of London traffic bringing its average speed down to 12 mph, Mail Rail remains as valuable as ever in easing the strain on London's streets and speeding the mail beneath them.

Chapter 10
Travelling Post Offices

*This is the night mail crossing
    the border
Bringing the cheque and the
    postal order
Letters for the rich, letters
    for the poor,
The shop at the corner and the girl
    next door.*

These are the opening lines of W H
Auden's poem, written for the
award-winning 1936 GPO documentary film *Night Mail*. The film —
still much in demand from the Post
Office Film and Video Unit – features
the Down Special TPO from London
Euston to Glasgow and Aberdeen.

In 1936 it was part of what had
become a comprehensive network.
There were more than 70 of these
rail-based mobile sorting offices in
which postal staff sorted mail as the

TPOs sped through the night, dropping off the sorted mail at points
along the way.

This was the heyday of the TPO.
World War Two brought the network
to a virtual standstill. By 1940 only
the Up and Down Specials (of Night
Mail fame) and the Great Western
TPO (linking Penzance and London
Paddington) were running. The TPOs
on these two routes remain the key
links in the network to this day.

After the war the distribution patterns for mail changed and only just
over half the pre-war routes were
restored. By 1975, the network comprised 48 regular TPOs, processing
some 400 million letters a year.

In 1988 the first major review of the
network since the war brought the
number of TPOs down to 35, though
four new routes were created, some

existing routes extended, others combined. The new streamlined network
handles 25 million more letters a year
than were handled in 1975.

The Down Special of Auden's poem
has remained throughout. Every
weekday evening its 12 empty
coaches still roll into Platform 2 at
Euston to signal the start of 105
minutes of bustling activity.

Streams of mail vans, bringing letters from all over London, drive on to
the platform to be unloaded straight
into the TPO. Sorting begins as the
packed train leaves the station and
the mail is bagged up again, ready to
be dropped off at stations en route or
at the two big Scottish cities.

*Letters of thanks, letters from
    banks,
Letters of joy from the girl and boy,*

Today's Night Mail: the modern TPO in its bright red Royal Mail livery speeds the first class letters across the country.

Receipted bills and invitations
To inspect new stock or visit
    relations,
And applications for situations,
And timid lovers' declarations ...

London staff work through the night as far as Carlisle, where they hand over to a Scottish crew. The Londoners lodge in Carlisle 'overday' and sort their way back to Euston on the Up Special that evening (in railway terms trains always travel down from, and up to, London).

Letters with holiday snaps to
    enlarge in,
Letters with faces scrawled on the
    margin,
Letters from uncles, cousins and
    aunts,
Letters to Scotland from the South
    of France ...

Above: The Down Special from London to Glasgow and Aberdeen being loaded at Euston in 1938.

Left: The TPO of the 1990s taking on mail at Euston. The new livery was introduced in 1986.

The origins of the railway TPO predate the Penny Black by a couple of years. Early in 1838 the Post Office used a converted horse-box to sort mail in transit on the Grand Junction Railway between Birmingham and Warrington.

But Rowland Hill had seen the advantages of sorting in transit as

The first purpose-built travelling post office, on the London and Birmingham railway.

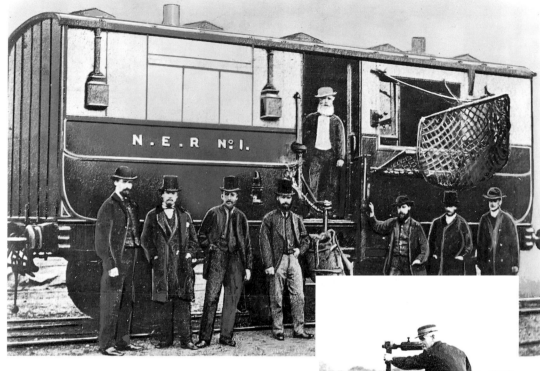

Above: The picture taken to mark the first TPO between York and Scarborough in 1881.

Right. The mail hangs waiting to be scooped up at Thirsk around 1900.

early as 1826. He had proposed that a special horse-drawn mail coach be adapted so that the guard could sort and tax the letters inside it.

This never happened, but a Post Office surveyor, Frederick Karstadt, worked on the idea and 11 years later some mail was being sorted at stops along the mail coach route. By this time the railways were expanding and Karstadt was able to turn to this more promising method of transport for mobile sorting. It was he who planned that first TPO in the converted horse-box.

It was an instant success. Never before had sorting and delivery been so effective and swift. By 9 April 1838 the first purpose-built sorting car-

riage was in use. It travelled on the London and Birmingham Railway from Euston to Bletchley where the sorted mail was switched to horse-drawn mail coaches.

In November that year, as the railways extended further north-west, the Post Office introduced day and night sorting carriages between London and Preston. This was the start and, as the railways expanded, the travelling post office network grew with them.

Sorting apart, mail had travelled by rail from the pioneer days of the railways: there are records of mail bags being carried on the Liverpool and Manchester Railway soon after it opened in 1830. Railway mail coaches were rapidly replacing the horse-drawn variety.

Here was the future of mail transport, and a firm commitment was needed from the railways management to ensure the safe and efficient passage of the Royal Mail. After much discussion and an Act of Parliament, the Post Office gained wide powers which it still holds: it could put mail on any train, request trains to run at its convenience, call for special rolling stock ... Railway post offices, as they were called until 1928, had become an integral and influential part of the British railway network.

In the early days the exchange of mail along the route was a hazardous business. The train merely slowed

Inside the Great Northern TPO, the latest design at the time, around 1900.

and the bags were hurled out by hand. Trickier still, mail was collected from a ten-foot pole held aloft.

Judgement, timing and nerve were not always up to the task. A hard canvas bag hurled from a train was a missile to avoid rather than catch, and the TPO staff, for their part, needed to keep a wary eye on the end of the pole. So there was some relief when trackside apparatus began to replace the jousting and bag-hurling contests.

But life on the early TPOs was still hard and hazardous. Between 1860 and 1867, there were 28 accidents in which TPO men were seriously injured or killed. Fumes from the oil lamps and wax for sealing the bags caused sickness and affected the brain. Early retirements were common. Few could take TPO work for more than about 15 years.

The railside catching device, intro-

Now you see it, now you don't. A sequence showing wayside mail picked up at speed.

duced on a regular basis in 1852, lasted with very little modification for more than 100 years. The mail was packed in stout leather pouches that could weigh up to 60lb. To collect them in transit, the TPO was fitted with a net which could extend outwards to pick up mail hanging from the successor to the ten-foot pole – a ten-foot lineside standard.

Pouches leaving the TPO were similarly hung from an arm extending three feet from the side of the carriage, to be caught in a waiting net. There might be up to four of these arms on a carriage, the opening to each one guarded by a safety bar to prevent staff from falling out while hanging the pouch.

Though less hazardous than the early operations, it still called for skill and timing. A mistake could seriously damage both the mail and the equipment: in the first quarter of this century the Post Office had a printed label to attach to delicate-looking packages telling recipients that it had been diverted from the usual route as 'it appeared to be too fragile for transfer by mail apparatus.'

High-speed trains, and changes in postal distribution methods, gradually brought the end of these mobile mail exchange techniques. The last exchange took place at Penrith on 3 October 1971. The Up Special, to London, made the pick up and the North Western TPO Night Down hung out the last despatch. Trains now stop at Penrith instead.

Right: Stark against the sky, the last bag awaits the final pick-up at Penrith on 3 October 1971.

The Men behind Night Mail

Night Mail – the poster for the GPO Film Unit's illustrious documentary. The unit, formed in 1933 with a young and talented team, quickly built its reputation for making outstanding films and for fostering talent. During the war it became the Crown Film Unit turning out documentaries to help the war effort.

Today the same spirit lives on in the Post Office Film and Video Unit, whose "Men of Letters" won gold awards at the British and American Film Festivals in 1986. A wide selection of Post Office films from the 1930s to the present day is in continuous demand for sale or hire to schools, clubs and film buffs throughout Britain and abroad.

Chapter 11
The Post Office at War

E laborate plans were made to ensure that the centenary year of uniform penny postage was memorable. They largely came to nought, but 1940 could hardly have been more memorable.

It saw the Battle of Britain reach a devastating climax. The blitz on London began in June and grew in intensity until, over a three-month period, there were raids every night. On one September night alone, 23 London post offices were hit. In another raid Mount Pleasant sorting office was bombed and set fiercely ablaze. At one time or another every London railway station was blasted out of action.

Through it all, the mail was deli-

Right: Mount Pleasant in ruins after a direct hit on 18 June 1943.

vered – some of it collected from pillar boxes dug out of the rubble – and post office customers were served, often from makeshift temporary counters.

This was just one aspect, briefly glimpsed, of the Post Office at war. Dramas, tragedies, acts of heroism became commonplace in many parts of Britain, part of a great Post Office wartime tradition.

In the Crimean War, for instance, 11 postal staff served with the troops, ensuring that the Light Brigade and the rest of the expeditionary forces received their mail. The unit handled 450,000 letters a month.

The Boer War was a bigger operation. About ten officers and 500 men in South Africa handled some three-quarters of a million letters and parcels a week.

This again was dwarfed by World War One. Temporary wooden buildings in Regent's Park, put up to handle the military sorting operation, kept growing to keep pace with demand, becoming known as the biggest wooden building in the world. By 1915, 4,000 mail bags a day were being despatched to the Army's base post office in Le Havre, and over the Christmas periods the pressure was enormous. But the mail was carried

Above: A Post Office salvage squad removes a blitzed safe.

Right: Business as usual from a make-shift temporary post office.

through to the troops wherever they were.

Many of these soldiers were former Post Office staff. The exploits of the Post Office Rifles Regiment during 1914–18 are alone the subject of a book (*Terriers in the Trenches* by Charles Messenger), whose pages are full of stories of heroism.

During that time the two line battalions, constantly reinforced to refill the ranks, drew 12,000 men into the mayhem of that terrible campaign. More than half became casualties, with 1,800 killed and 4,500 wounded. Gallantry medals include one Victoria Cross, some 40 Military Crosses and 160 Military Medals.

World War Two brought a similar response. At the outbreak, or soon after, more than 70,000 staff joined up, of whom 3,800 gave their lives. On the Home Front more than 400 staff were killed. By the middle of the war more than a third of the 300,000 staff were in the forces. Another 75,000 joined the Home Guard.

As in World War One, women filled the gaps. There were 20,000 post-women (compared with 600 pre-war); others did sorting, counter work and van driving. Between them, in and out of uniform, Post Office staff

Above: The 1914–18 Army Postal Service at work.

Right: Lewisham post office – a typical scene at the height of the World War Two bombing.

earned more than 700 wartime honours.

The blitz brought the war to the Home Front as never before. To start with, there was the blackout. The glass roof at Mount Pleasant had to be permanently blacked out, so all wartime sorting had to be in artificial light. Outside, at night and before dawn, there was much groping around on delivery and, particularly, on station platforms.

In the blitz thousands of fan lights and front doors disappeared, and with them the house numbers. The Post Office had to appeal to people without a house number to chalk it up plainly to help the many inexperienced postmen and women.

The Post Office also became very concerned about wasting paper. Envelopes were reused, forms were sent out without envelopes and the public was even urged to save stamps by using the exact postage with one stamp rather than two. The stamps were even made in a lighter shade so that less dye was needed in the cancellation.

Right: Buried pillar boxes were a frequent problem during the blitz. But the mail was usually safely extracted and sent on its way. From a Ben Maile painting.

Women drivers and women grooms who drove the horse-drawn mail vans during the 1914–18 war.

Much vital war work was involved in distributing millions of ration books and information leaflets, issuing permits and allowances. The Post Office also collected and forwarded 20 million books and magazines for the forces.

Winston Churchill had given instructions that London and Home Counties post offices, and others in the regions, should keep a war diary. These accounts, mostly prepared by head postmasters, dealt with the dramas of those days with typical British understatement. For example:

"15 December 1942, Saxmundham, Aldeburgh post office, 1.15pm. The post office received a direct hit; completely demolished; four staff killed, three injured. Remainder of day's business continued at a town sub-office. Temporary premises secured at 8.30am on 16th. Counter service made available to the public ..."

And from Hastings, 11 April 1941:

"Shelling most part of the day; bombs from a single raider. Nothing to report apart from damage to the sorting office. Blast from near miss caused

Right: Directions for a newly recruited telegraph messenger during the blitz.

appreciable damage, but work interrupted only to a minor degree."

The World War Two equivalent of that 1914–18 wooden structure in Regent's Park was a former textile factory in Nottingham. All mail for the Army and the RAF was routed through this midlands Mount Pleasant, staffed mainly by women of the WRAC and former Post Office men in the Royal Engineers Postal Section.

They dealt with one million parcels, three million newspaper packets and many more millions of letters every week. The parcels and newspapers went by surface mail and the letters by air, which was a considerable burden on essential aircraft capacity. Could the load be lightened? Yes it could – by transferring each letter to microfilm.

A special form was created, the airgraph. It was rather like an unsealed aerogram. Everything – home address, message and destination – was written on one side of the paper. This went to London's East Central sorting office where it was numbered by handstamp, so that should the microfilm be lost in transit it could be rephotographed and sent again.

After being sorted, each batch of

Right: This poster helped to attract 20 million books and magazines for the forces.

Below: One of several posters that helped to attract 350 million airgraphs.

Airgraph forms being photographed.

Left: Airgraphs being stamped and numbered so they could be traced if the film was lost.

airgraphs was photographed one at a time by being dropped through a slit into a box containing a camera. A 100 ft strip of film coiled in a metal container weighed 5½ ounces and carried 1,700 letters. At the distant end the film was developed and enlarged on to sensitized paper, folded and automatically enclosed in a window envelope.

Airgraphs were first used from the Middle East in May 1941, and Queen Elizabeth, the present Queen Mother, wrote the first one back, to General Auchinleck, on 15 August. They finally extended as far as Australia, and when they were withdrawn in July 1945 more than 350 million had been sent, weighing a total of 50 tons compared with 4,500 tons had they been letters.

For correspondence with prisoners-of-war, an airmail letter card was introduced early in the war. Mail to and from Germany and Italy was routed via Lisbon: there was good co-operation as our adversaries were equally keen that their countrymen held in Britain should receive mail from home.

There were two types of parcels: those sent personally to a prisoner from his home, and those made up by the Red Cross for general distribution. These last were sent to the International Red Cross in Geneva which distributed them to 20 million prisoners of all nationalities.

In little over four years the Post Office despatched more than 26 mil-

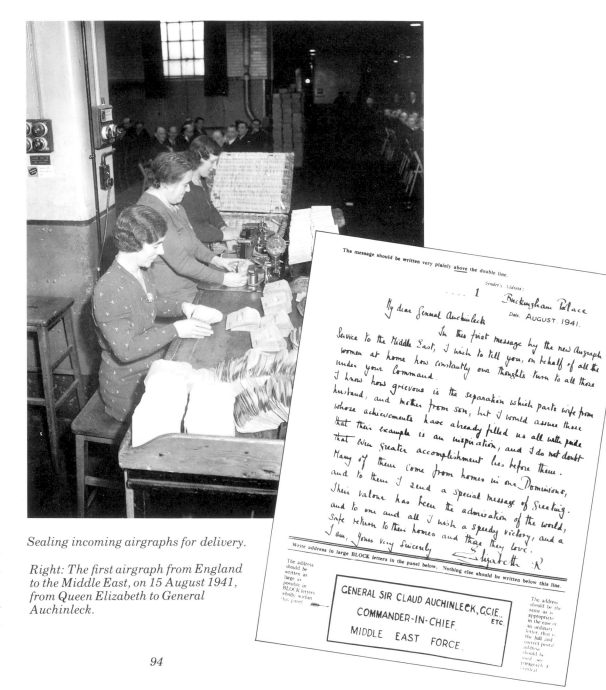

Sealing incoming airgraphs for delivery.

Right: The first airgraph from England to the Middle East, on 15 August 1941, from Queen Elizabeth to General Auchinleck.

Red Cross parcels for prisoners of war being despatched from Mount Pleasant in September 1941.

lion parcels. For one batch alone, 17 special trains were needed to carry the parcels to the dockside.

So for the Post Office, on all fronts, it was a busy war. But before the blitz began there was just time to mark the centenary of uniform penny postage. On 6 May 1940, exactly 100 years after the Penny Black was introduced, a special series of stamps was issued. Valued from a halfpenny to three pence, each stamp featured the heads of Queen Victoria and George VI.

There was also a Postage Stamp Centenary Dinner at which the Postmaster-General, W S Morrison, commented on how the war was affecting the Post Office and on the irony of celebrating the anniversary of 'a victory of peace from which the whole world has benefited.'

Chapter 12
The Post Office Takes Up Philately

The Swinging Sixties, heyday of the Beatles, of peace campaigns and Flower Power, was also the decade that saw the Post Office take up philately.

From the early days of stamps, postal authorities round the world had realised there was revenue to be made (if not earned!) from this universally popular hobby. Stamps of all kinds and shapes began to appear. But for more than a century the British Post Office remained aloof, concentrating on providing a postal service rather than a philatelic one.

But as the popularity of stamp collecting grew and major businesses, not the least of them in Britain, were thriving on the hobby, the world's foremost Post Office climbed down from its pedestal. It owed it to the public at large, as well as philatelists,

This sheet of Penny Black stamps, held at the Post Office's National Postal Museum, is the only complete sheet in existence. It is the 1 April 1840 proof of the first printing plate, at that stage unfinished. It lacks the letters in the bottom corners of each stamp, showing its position on the sheet.

The original master die from which all the stamps – Penny Black and Penny Red – were made up to 1857. Another National Postal Museum treasure.

to offer a service. After all, the extra revenue would help to offset the costs of collection and delivery, so everyone benefited.

Post Office philately was born on May Day 1963. That was the date the Philatelic Bureau opened alongside GPO Headquarters, ready to serve the stamp collectors of the world.

Soon afterwards the Post Office was further encouraged to treasure its wares when it was given a stamp collection of its own. The benefactor was the eminent philatelist Reginald Phillips who had amassed one of the two finest collections of Victorian stamps in existence, the other being the royal collection at Buckingham Palace. All Mr Phillips asked was that the Post Office hold it in trust for the nation.

The result was the National Postal Museum. It opened at London's Chief Post Office, King Edward Building, in 1966.

Rowland Hill's statue in King Edward Street might have allowed itself a smile. On one side of the street was GPO Headquarters; a few yards to the south, the Philatelic Bureau, serving the world's most popular hobby; below, the underground railway Hill had advocated to speed mail across

The first first-day cover: a letter sheet posted on the first day stamps were legally used – 6 May 1840. A piece of a similar letter sheet, posted ahead of time on 2 May, the day after the stamps went on sale, fetched £50,000 at a London auction in November 1989.

Top right: A typical Penny Black stamp with the original red cancellation, used for ten months. The letter G indicated that the stamp was in the seventh row on the complete sheet, and the L shows it was 12th from the left (the last vertical row). The value of the Penny Black varies widely. As they were cut from the sheet with scissors, the amount of white border is one factor. a poor example can fetch about £40.

The Wyon City Medal, engraved by William Wyon to mark Queen Victoria's accession visit to the City of London in 1837. Drawings of the head, showing the Queen at 18, were used for all stamps during her reign.

All three items are at the National Postal Museum.

the capital; and opposite, a postal museum founded on the stamps he had introduced to the world, many of them now priceless.

The Philatelic Bureau was quickly in action, producing 'First Day of Issue' postmarks for the Paris Postal Conference stamp of 7 May 1963. Nine days later, for the National Nature Week issue, the bureau offered a First Day Cover service. There was more activity for the Lifeboat Conference and the Red Cross Centenary issues later that year.

Two other important developments followed:

■ in 1964 the Postmaster-General, Anthony Wedgwood Benn, set out the policy which has led to the current pattern of some seven or eight special issues a year;
■ in 1968 the Post Office Stamp Advisory Committee was formed to watch over the quality of British stamp design.

Before the sixties, British special stamps were a rare phenomenon. The first one appeared in 1924 to mark the British Empire Exhibition. Subsequently the occasion had to be either royal, postal, or very special indeed, such as the Victory stamps of 1946,

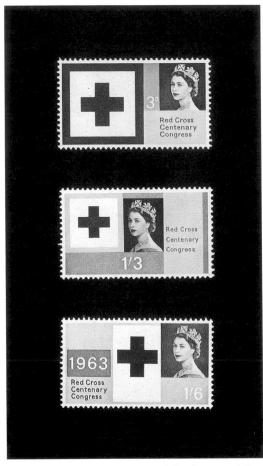

The Red Cross stamps, one of the first special issues handled by the Philatelic Bureau in 1963.

the 1948 Olympic Games in London, the 1951 Festival of Britain and the World Scout Jubilee Jamboree in 1957.

A relaxation of the policy was

reflected in the 1963 issues, and the guidelines set out the following year were clearly prompted by the need to formalize and clarify what was already under way. The current criteria are little changed from 1964. Topics chosen must:

■ commemorate important anniversaries;
■ celebrate events of national and international importance;
■ reflect the British contribution to world affairs, particularly the Commonwealth and Europe, in a variety of fields of activity including the arts and sciences;
■ show the many and varied aspects of Britain and the British way of life;
■ extend public patronage to the arts by encouraging the development of miniscule art;
■ fit in with the Post Office's commercial targets for philately.

A few conventions have also developed with experience. These include avoiding any topic which may be controversial or cause offence; no living person, other than Royalty, to be depicted; anniversaries normally to be 50 (or multiples of 50) years; recent past and possible future subjects to be taken into account to

Britain's first special stamps, issued for the British Empire Exhibition in 1924 and again, with a fresh date, when the exhibition reopened in 1925.

The early special issues had to be very special, such as the Victory stamps of 1946, and, overleaf the London Olympics in 1948 (top left), the 1951 Festival of Britain (lower left) and the World Scout Jubilee Jamboree in 1957 (right).

ensure balance and variety year by year; and each year to have a variety of subjects.

These guidelines have proved invaluable in sifting through the hundreds of suggestions the Post Office receives each year. These are first pruned down to a short-list, then philatelists and the general public have their say through representative discussion groups.

The Stamp Advisory Committee's task is to advise the Post Office on the design implications of the subjects to be included, on the artists to be invited to submit designs, to brief those artists and to advise on the designs to be submitted to the Queen for approval.

The committee has 12 non-Post-Office members – mostly eminent designers but including two lay members and two philatelists. The two Post Office members are the head of design and the general manager of stamps and philately, who is the committee chairman.

Detailed planning of the stamp programme begins about 18 months in advance. Several designers are commissioned for each issue and all are first briefed on the operational needs. The Queen's portrait is essen-

tial because it identifies the stamp as British (Britain remains the only postal authority in the world that does not have to put the name of the country on its stamps).

It is the committee's task to ensure that British stamps maintain their leading place in the world of stamp design and production. Their success in this is clearly shown by the international honours British stamps have earned over the years.

Once the stamps are approved, printed and distributed, the great majority do the job Rowland Hill envisaged, providing a receipt for postage paid. The philatelic side is just a tiny fraction of the total, but it has grown enormously to meet the demand at home and abroad.

The Philatelic Bureau, which moved to Edinburgh in 1966, now has a staff of more than 200, a computer system involving 40 visual display units and specially designed stamp handling and packaging equipment to deal with the millions of orders from collectors worldwide.

Top right: The Ballerina and Harlequin stamps from the 1982 British Theatre set each won separate awards in worldwide competitions in Italy in 1983. The Mary and Jesus stamp from the 1984 Christmas set (right) won both these same awards in 1985.

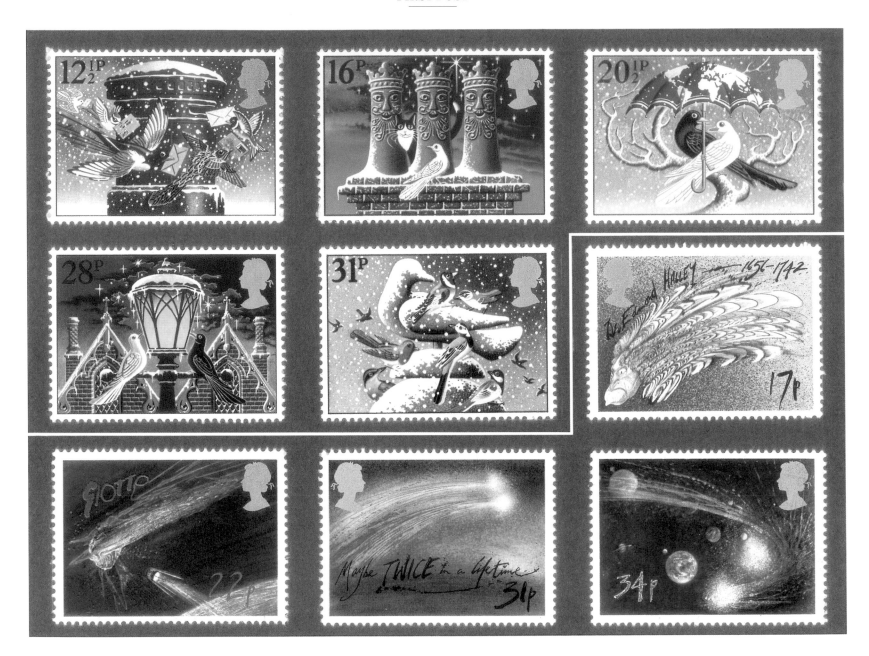

The 1983 Christmas issue (far left, top) won international honours in Austria. Back home, three sets were honoured in the graphics section of the 1987 BBC Design Awards: Halley's Comet (1986) and, this page, Films (1985) and Flowers (1987).

As well as a great variety of stamps, the bureau has a comprehensive catalogue covering all kinds of publications and stationery of interest to collectors, much of which is also on sale at specialist philatelic counters at main post offices.

The *British Philatelic Bulletin*, launched from the bureau in London in 1963, now has 50,000 subscribers. The bureau also distributes the *British Postmark Bulletin* to some 2,000 postmark collectors.

Children's interest in the hobby is catered for through the Stamp Bug Club which, with some 62,000 members, is probably the biggest club of its kind in the world. Members receive the club magazine, *Stamp Bug News*, every two months, and each year they get a membership card, calendar, stamp album and specially designed first day cover envelopes.

Once a year in December the bureau takes on a dual role, becoming Reindeerland. All children's letters addressed to Father Christmas are sent to the bureau, where the staff respond on his behalf with a colourful card from Santa.

The Philatelic Bureau, 20 Brandon Street, Edinburgh. The building itself appears on a 29p special stamp in 1990.

Left: The Duke of York with a display version of one of the four high value stamps based on his photographs of famous castles, introduced into the range in 1988.

Chapter 13
Machines to Sort the Mail

Even postal mechanisation can be traced back to Rowland Hill. His uniform penny post was founded on the fact that distance was not the main cost factor in postal distribution. The costs are at each end – in collection, franking, sorting for despatch at the start, then final sorting and delivery.

The ideal – the dream – was to have machinery that could read the address once, then sort it at both ends of its journey, right down to the correct house sequence for the postman. In the 1990s that dream is heading for reality.

The big breakthrough came in 1966 when the Post Office added a new element to every address in the country – the postcode. At the time there were 18 million of them. Today there are nearer 24 million.

Inside the revolving segregator handy-sized letters drop through the slits while the more bulky mail tumbles out at the bottom for human attention.

It was a considerable clerical and promotional task, and the decision to undertake it, in the face of some public resistance, was bold and far-

sighted. The fact that today's Post Office is able to cope with well in excess of 50 million letters a day – involving an increase of 40% in a decade – is made possible by automatic handling and sorting at 80 mechanised letter offices.

The problem of getting machines to handle the mail starts when the assortment of letters and packets is unloaded in the sorting office. What kind of machine can produce order from this chaos? The Post Office found the answer in the 1950s: a mechanical dynamic duo called Alf and the segregator.

The segregator is a large angled cylinder which rotates, letting the handy-sized letters slip out so they can be stacked for Alf. All the packets are spewed out at the end of the cylinder for human attention. If the

This is Alf. Letters loaded on the left go through a maze of pulleys and belts and emerge in regimental order – and in first and second class divisions.

power back into the system. Incoming letters and packets are dropped onto a long table for postmen to pick up and put, right way round, onto one of three conveyor belts – for first class letters, second class letters, and for packets. The conveyors take the handy mail off for automatic franking and stacking, and the packets for human attention.

The third and latest method went on trial at Northampton in 1989. A smaller, more efficient version of the segregator/Alf system, it can handle 27,000 letters an hour, about twice

This facer-canceller took over from Alf and segregator. Note the handy first and second class conveyors.

segregator cannot catch a letter, Alf cannot handle it either.

Alf, the automatic letter facer, starts by getting the handy-sized mail – which is the majority of it – all facing the same way. He does this by detecting phosphor put on all stamps for his benefit. He also sorts the mail into first and second class, rejecting any unstamped letters. Alf and his segregator were installed in major sorting offices during the late 1960s and early 1970s.

The next development – the facer-canceller table – brought more man-the speed of the facing and cancelling process. It can also separate typed from hand-written mail.

All this machinery, sophisticated though it is, has not touched on the important job – sorting each individual letter to its destination.

The traditional manual sorting frame has 48 pigeon holes, the highest number a man can reasonably reach. It is tiring work. What is more, 48 selections are not enough so still more sorting is needed.

The first step towards mechanising that process came in October 1935 when two Dutch machines were installed for trials in Brighton. The Transorma, as it was called, had five operator positions and could sort to 250 destinations.

Each operator sat at a numeric keyboard, picked up the letters with one hand and punched in a code with the other. A moving belt carried the letters to the appropriate pigeon holes. The two Transormas did a useful operational job through to 1968 and provided valuable information for further development. The Transorma had one major snag. The operator had to work at the rhythm of the machine. He worked better at his own speed, quick for easy familiar codes, slower

The very latest machinery for turning mail bag chaos into sorting-ready order. Though much smaller than their predecessors, the new generation segregator, feeding the contemporary Alf, are between them 36 feet long. They are also more efficient.

for more obscure, illegible ones. The Royal Mail never cracked that one. The only solution was to have one-operator sorting machines.

A single-operator version of the Transorma, for smaller offices, went on trial at Bath in 1955. It was a big

advance on its parent machine. The layout of the conveyor was much more compact, and the machine picked up each letter for the operator to see and code.

A second machine installed later at Southampton linked up with Alf and

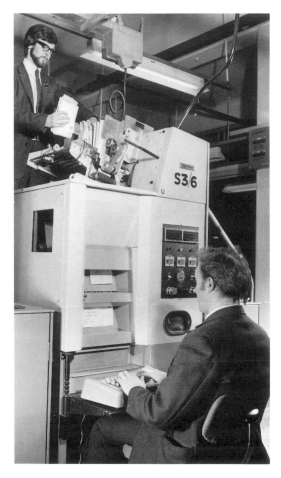

Far left: The very first code-sorting machine, the Transorma. The main snag was that the codes had to be keyed at one pace.

Left: The first coding desks developed from the Norwich trials. They are loaded from above, with two envelopes on view.

Above: The modern coding desk. Letters travel across the eye.

his segregator. Between 1958 and 1960 the Post Office bought and distributed 20 more for wider trials, ten machines to individual offices and ten to the office that was to be the test bed for advanced code sorting – Norwich.

But not just yet. The Post Office began to see the advantages of using letters instead of numbers. They would be easier for the operator to remember.

Experiments led to two five-character codes, one for the town, the other for the street. They used the first three and last two letters of the post town – BRION for BRIghtON, ELYLY for Ely; and the first two and last two letters of the street name plus R for road, L for lane, etc – SIERS for Silver Street, FOUEA for Fortescue Avenue.

What about Brighton and Bridlington? Well, the Post Office decided, nothing is perfect and the 5% ambi-

The most common sorting machine in the late 1980s, handling up to 16,000 letters and hour. The postwoman is taking sorted mail from one of the compartments while (right) mail to be sorted is being fed into the back of another machine.

guity could be predicted and catered for. New typewriter keyboards were installed on the single-position sorting machines at Southampton (SOUON) and worked well.

But it was just a one-sorting operation. The Post Office wanted more. It wanted an address on the envelope that a machine could read.

The answer – to separate the keyboard and sorting operation – killed two birds with one stone. The keyboard would mark the envelope so

the machine – any machine, right through the system – could read it. The bonus: any number of operators, keying at their own speed, could code letters for one sorting machine.

But what did machines prefer to read? After much experiment, Post Office researchers came up with coded phosphor dots. A test rig was installed at Luton in October 1959 and, after a successful trial, two coding desks and one sorter were brought into use on live mail the following year.

The next step was the big one. The need for postcodes for every address was becoming apparent and this involved a new ingredient – the public. Without public co-operation the dream of a fully automatic system would remain just a dream.

The people of Norwich and district became the guinea pigs of the postcoding process. They got the first experimental postcodes in 1959, and mechanical trials began there in 1966. By the end of that year the first of the modern postcodes were introduced at Croydon. They spread from there throughout the country, finishing with the re-coding of the Norwich area in 1974.

The current postcode – the key to the dream – consists of two groups of

letters and figures. This dual code, translated into phosphor dots on the envelope just once at the start, takes the letter through the system.

The first group of letters are read by the outward sorting machine, which gets the letter to its sorting office of destination. There, an identical machine reads the second group of three letters to sort to part of a street or even an individual address.

Before the Norwich trials there were sorting offices in about 1700 towns and the Norwich experiment was based on outward codes for all of them. But this would have been an uneconomic use of machines, so the decision was made to have about 120 big mechanised letter sorting offices and allocate the codes on this basis (though the 120 figure was later reduced).

Croydon became the first mechanised letter office to use the new codes. By the summer of 1970, 34 coding desks and 11 sorting machines had been brought into use.

Similar equipment was also going into London's East Central, Southampton and Newport sorting offices. Growth continued over the next two years; then in 1973 the postmen's union, worried about manning

The latest sorting machine, the E40, sorts up to 32,000 letters an hour.

arrangements, called a halt, refusing to work on the new machines.

It was a setback for the whole programme, not least the public element, at a time when the Post Office was working hard to get postcodes more widely used. The dispute lasted until 1975.

Meanwhile the Post Office had produced a new type of coding desk, Easy View. The letters passed horizontally before the operator so he could see several at a time, and he could control the speed of the letters. This is basi-

cally the coding machine in use today.

On the sorting front, speeds have doubled twice since the early 1970s. The first machines could sort 7,500 letters an hour. A new machine tried first at Redhill, Surrey, in 1975, successfully sorted at up to 16,000 an hour. Within the next decade it was installed in 80 offices.

Reading was the test bed of the latest machine, the E40, capable of sorting at up to 32,000 an hour: in 1989 the Post Office ordered 16 more.

The Post Office's gentle persuasion

and encouragement of the public to use the postcode is finally gaining the co-operation it planned for. Some three-quarters of all letters are now postcoded, and the gradual inclusion of the codes in British Telecom's 128 phone books, from 1989, will make them more readily accessible.

But the biggest breakthrough of all is in optical character recognition – a machine that automatically reads the postcode on the envelope and adds the appropriate phosphor codes for the sorting machine to read.

The first OCR machine went on trial at London's Mount Pleasant in the early 1980s. Around 1987–8 17 machines were installed and operating; 29 more were ordered 12 months later. These machines read typed and printed postcodes. The next stage is to get them to read handwritten postcodes. Good progress is being made on the last barrier. The postal dream is becoming a reality.

There is just one aspect of the service the Royal Mail has not worked out how to mechanise: getting the letter up the garden path, the tower block stairs, through farmyard gates ... For that job nothing beats a postman or postwoman.

The optical character recognition machine in the foreground reads typed or printed addresses and adds the phosphor dots for machine sorting. Unlike the coding desk operators in the background, it cannot read handwriting – yet.

Chapter 14
Postbus – the Modern Mail Coach

Mrs May Lewis of Llangurig, Montgomeryshire, was delighted when, on Monday 20 February 1967, she was able to travel from her village home into the nearby town, Llanidloes, courtesy of the Royal Mail. Mrs Lewis was one of seven passengers on Britain's first postbus, or postal minibus as it was originally called.

Despite heavy rain, the villagers turned out in force to see postman-driver Stanley Owen collect the fares, issue the tickets and, at 12.15pm, set off on the first passenger-carrying run.

Mr Owen had driven out from Llanidloes that morning, delivering the mail as usual. On the 15-minute

Stanley Owen, the first postbus driver, helps passengers aboard his Llangurig/Llanidloes postbus.

journey back with his passengers he made two stops to pick up mail. At 4.15pm he made the round trip once more, this time bringing the passengers back home and continuing his evening collections.

For the villagers of Llangurig, previously without any mid-week bus service, the Royal Mail's new service was a lifeline. For the Post Office, however, it was an experiment. Mr Neal, the Post Office Director in Wales, said at the inaugural run that 'it is possible other routes will be considered.'

They were. On Monday 23 October that year the Devon village of Luppitt became the first English village to get a postbus – into Honiton – and a week later a service began in Cumbria between Martindale and Penrith.

Scotland's first postbus came seven months later, on Tuesday 4 June 1968, with a service linking Innerwick and Dunbar, in East Lothian.

These were the four pioneer postbus routes, rekindling a service that began with the packet boat and continued with the horse-drawn mail coach. Like its predecessors, the postbus's prime purpose was to carry the Royal Mail at times that suited the service, but if passengers wanted to

Postman-driver George Wilkinson helps passengers aboard his postbus on the scenic Duddon Valley route in the Lake District.

travel at those times they could be sure of a reliable, regular and punctual ride.

The Post Office had been a little doubtful about breaking its modern rule that members of the public could not travel on Royal Mail vehicles, but

solved the security problem with a 30-cubic-foot mail locker built into the back of the minibus.

Mr Neal's initial caution was justified, however. None of these four routes made a profit, and no further progress was made until after 1969, when the Post Office left the Civil Service and became a nationalised industry. This constitutional change transformed the situation, opening the way for Government grants and local authority subsidies that encour-aged more routes to be established.

In 1972, eight more opened in Scotland, and south-east England got its first postbus, between Crundale and Canterbury. The following year, the Goulceby-Louth service, in the Lincolnshire Wolds, became the first in the north-east.

By the end of 1973 there were 31 routes; 52 more opened in the next two years and a further 77 in the decade to 1985. The total in 1990: 183 postbus routes – 145 in Scotland, 26 in England and 12 in Wales.

For thousands of people in rural communities the postbus has become a vital link with the outside world. For tourists and lovers of the country-side the link is the other way, offering delightful journeys to remote corners of Britain.

That first English route between Honiton and Luppitt – now postbus route number one – offers a 46-mile circular tour of attractive corners of Devon.

Another popular route takes in the scenic Northumbrian coast from Chathill to Bamburgh. In summer, postbus passengers can also take motorboat trips to the Farne Islands to see the grey seals and sea-birds.

But the unofficial postbus capital

A young passenger boards the postbus on the Isle of Barra in the Outer Hebrides. There were 145 Scottish postbus routes in 1989.

The Chathill/Bamburgh route, serving the Northumbrian Coast, with tourist attractions like Bamburgh Castle.

has to be Inverness, whose extensive and rugged postal area includes 50 postbus routes which between them cover nearly a million miles of roads and carry more than 30,000 passengers through some of Scotland's grandest scenery.

Further routes are likely, not only in the Inverness area but throughout the country. Increasingly, district head postmasters and local authorities are getting together to see where the Royal Mail's postal transport can be adapted to carry people along with the mail, and there is plenty of scope for expansion.

As it approaches its silver jubilee, the 20th century version of the mail coach looks set for a more permanent place in Post Office history.

Chapter 15
The Post Office Today

Today, the Royal Mail is the largest of the Post Office businesses. It is vastly different from the one Rowland Hill revamped in 1840. But the great postal reformer's basic principle remains: there is still a uniform price for delivery to any part of the country, no matter how remote.

The cost of postage also compares favourably, considering that a manual worker's wage in 1840 could send 264 letters while a similar average weekly wage in 1990 would buy 1,000 first class stamps.

INFORMATION TECHNOLOGY: Concept 2000, modern hub of the Post Office's Information Technology department at Farnborough, Hampshire. The department grew three-fold in 1989 just as it had over the previous two years. Tracking and tracing mail, planning better mail routes, a voice and data network for the Post Office, counter automation for Post Office Counters and keeping track of TV licences are typical projects.

In the 1990s, everyone, business customers or private letter writers, in rural areas or city centres, has access to communication at low cost. The Royal Mail collects from 100,000 pillar boxes throughout the country as well as from thousands of individual businesses. Indeed, business mail now accounts for over 80 per cent of letters posted, with new services such as Mailsort – which gives firms a discount for pre-sorting their mail – introduced to meet the needs of major customers.

When Rowland Hill first introduced uniform postage in 1840, letter writing was largely a privilege of the rich, educated few, and the Royal Mail handled some 76 million letters a year. Today, the figure is well over 13,000 million – almost as many in a day as were being posted in an entire year in Victorian times. And the daily task of Britain's postal service bears no comparison with the delivery of newspapers or milk because, unlike a bottle of milk or a newspaper, each letter is a unique, personalised item – of any shape or size – which might be going to any one of 24 million addresses throughout the country.

As late as the 1960s the Post Office was still a part of the Civil Service. In

This special stamp issue in 1979 marked the centenary of the death of Sir Rowland Hill.

1969 it became a public corporation. This change brought a new name. Those three famous initials, GPO, passed into the history books. The new title: The Post Office.

The next major change came 12 years later, in 1981, when the postal and telecommunications sides went their separate ways, and the latter were subsequently privatised as British Telecom.

RESEARCH: David Evans, a Post Office research engineer, at work on the revolutionary ink-jet printer that uses a unique phosphorescent ink to print codes on envelopes for machine sorting. The development, in the mid-1980s, earned him a gold medal award for engineering excellence. Safeglide, a spiral chute development for parcels and now also in demand for other uses such as airport baggage handling, is another example of Post Office research expertise.

Since then the trend has been to give the three main postal businesses – Royal Mail, Parcelforce and Post Office Counters – greater flexibility to meet the individual needs of their customers.

In 1986 the traditional all-purpose management structure, with head postmasters responsible for all three postal services, was swept away. Instead, each business set up the organisation that best suited its needs.

Royal Mail Letters, still by far the biggest unit, created 64 district offices reporting to four territorial headquarters – in Edinburgh (North), Manchester (West) and two in London (London and East).

Royal Mail Parcels – now retitled Parcelforce – scrapped the regional tier altogether, organising its 31 parcel concentration offices into 12 districts, with the district managers reporting direct to Parcels' Headquarters.

Post Office Counters set up 32 district offices and has three outstationed HQ units, in Leeds (North), Birmingham (West), and London (London and East).

The other major Post Office business, Girobank, had become a public company the year before.

The managing directors of the individual businesses became accountable to the chairman both for the running of their business and for operating within the overall Post Office policy.

HEALTH: Occupational health has a high priority in the Post Office. This is one of two Medibuses and there is also a travelling Roadshow, all of which tour offices giving health checks and advice. In 1988–9 the Post Office also launched a programme of cancer screening, available to its 35,000 women staff.

All three postal businesses continue to rely on shared central services, the principal ones being Information Technology, Research and Development, Purchasing and Supply and Occupational Health.

Collecting and recording television licence fees and chasing evaders, long a Post Office responsibility, also be-

TELEVISION LICENSING: The records of more than 19 million television licences are kept here at Bristol. Since it became a separate entity within the Post Office Corporation, Television Licensing has greatly reduced licence evasion. A specialist nationwide team backed by computerised records achieved a 14% drop in evasion in its first 12 months, and the downward trend has continued.

came a separate business entity: the National Television Licensing Organisation, with its Records office in Bristol and a network of 57 licence enquiry offices.

The reorganisation left Royal Mail Letters free to develop services for its customers and to concentrate on the formidable task of delivering 54 million letters a day, about half of them first class overnight. It also began to

concentrate on becoming a customer-led business, listening and responding to customer demands.

As part of this strategy, during 1988–9 the Royal Mail changed the way it measured the reliability of its service. It introduced independent 'pillar box to doormat' measurement and scrapped national averages.

Also, early in 1989, all households in the Newcastle and Darlington postal districts received a booklet telling them which post to catch for a high assurance of first class delivery in different parts of the country: 8.30am for the Outer Hebrides, noon for Northern Ireland and the West Country, 5.45pm for London, Bristol, North Wales and a wide local area, etc.

Since then every household in each district throughout the country has been provided with its own booklet, so everyone will know when to post first class letters to catch the trains and planes for next-day delivery anywhere in the UK.

Another positive response to customer demand came in November 1989 with the return, after an absence of 13 years, of Sunday collections. Edinburgh, Northern Ireland, Newcastle, Darlington and Cardiff were the first postal districts in a rolling

TRAINING: The Post Office has been one of the largest supporters of the Youth Training Scheme, and thousands of youngsters have turned their YTS experience into a full time job. The YTS is one aspect of a busy training programme co-ordinated centrally but now increasingly devolved to local management to ensure the training meets the specific needs of the businesses.

programme to restore Sunday collections in all districts during 1990.

British inland postal prices remain among the cheapest in Europe. Yet the British Post Office of today is one of the few postal authorities in the world that consistently makes a profit. Its decade of subsidy-free profit during the 1980s was unequalled throughout the EEC.

The development of the Post Office

SUPPLY: The Swindon depot of the Post Office Supply department. The department buys and distributes everything from millions of forms and other stationery to uniforms and vehicles, using its £350 million a year buying power to make targeted savings for the Letters, Counters and Parcels businesses as well as the corporate centre. The complex is also the home of the Research department.

from Civil Service department to a nationwide business covering a group of major specialist service industries has taken the wheel full circle.

The Royal Mail that Rowland Hill transformed in 1840 is once again, in the 1990s, able to specialise in that prime task.

After 150 years of spectacular development the British Royal Mail remains a leader in the increasingly complex postal world, and as it looks ahead to the 21st century it is in good shape to maintain that lead.

It is also a more flexible organisation, ready and able to listen – and respond – to the changing demands of its customers.

The Post Office of the 1990s – responding to customers' needs. Postman-driver Jim Lunan helps a passenger off his postbus beside the post office at Aboyne, between Balmoral and Aberdeen.

By air mail
Par avion

Index

Another Mail Rail train is sent on its subterranean way from London's Mount Pleasant.